Praise for

BE BAD FIRST
and Erika Andersen

"Erika Andersen shares a secret: competence is overrated. Fun to read and quite powerful...highly recommended."

—Seth Godin, author of *Your Turn*

"If the road to success is paved with mistakes well handled, then the journey of life is won by courageously choosing to stumble first in order to set distance records later. In *Be Bad First*, Erika Andersen lovingly guides us through the confidence-building steps necessary to master the part of growing up that doesn't benefit adults: a natural fear of failing to measure up."

—Danny Meyer, CEO of Union Square Hospitality Group and author of *Setting the Table: The Transforming Power of Hospitality in Business*

"In *Be Bad First*, Erika Andersen offers leadership strategies for the ever-changing business landscape that are essential for anyone trying to navigate it."

—Doug Herzog, president, Viacom Music & Entertainment Group

"I learned early in my career that whatever you are good at today will be old news tomorrow. As described in *Be Bad First*, responding well to this truth requires building specific mental skills. The book clearly shows you how to do that so you can stay in front of the pack with confidence no matter what. Read this book every year to sustain your success over time."

—Dr. Marcia Reynolds, author of *The Discomfort Zone: How Leaders Turn Difficult Conversations into Breakthroughs*

"Change is the new norm and with *Be Bad First*, Erika Andersen demonstrates how we all can be more agile and adaptive. She breaks down how to acquire new skills and knowledge quickly in order to thrive in today's fast-paced world."

—Maryam Banikarim, global chief marketing officer, Hyatt Hotels Corporation

"Erika Andersen exposes some of your darkest secrets, bringing them to light in a way that helps you realize it's not only okay to *Be Bad First*, but absolutely necessary for the learning process that leads to sustainable performance."

—Susan Fowler, author of *Why Motivating People Doesn't Work ... and What Does*

"Whatever it is you *have* to learn or *want* to learn, Erika's latest book shows you the way to open yourself to becoming all you can be."

—Dr. Jeff Tanner, dean, Strome College of Business, Old Dominion University

"We're often held back from trying new things, in both our personal and professional lives, by the fear that we're not going to be good at them. I love how Erika Andersen's *Be Bad First* gives leaders the confidence to experiment in the spirit of innovation—then quickly move on to greatness."

—Beth Comstock, vice chair, GE

"To succeed in today's rapidly changing world, you've constantly got to think and act in brand-new ways. Erika offers a fresh approach in clear, practical terms ... to get to 'good' or 'great,' you can't be afraid to *Be Bad First*."

—Bonnie Hammer, chairman, NBCUniversal Cable Entertainment Group

BE BAD
FIRST

BE BAD FIRST

Get Good at Things *FAST*
to Stay Ready for the Future

Erika Andersen

bibliomotion
inc.

First published by Bibliomotion, Inc.
39 Harvard Street
Brookline, MA 02445
Tel: 617-934-2427
www.bibliomotion.com

Printed in the United States of America

Library of Congress Cataloging-in-Publication Data

Names: Andersen, Erika, author.
Title: Be bad first : get good at things fast to stay ready for the future / Erika Andersen.
Description: Brookline, MA : Bibliomotion, Inc., [2016] | Includes bibliographical references and index.
Identifiers: LCCN 2015038239| ISBN 9781629561080 (hardcover : alk. paper) | ISBN 9781629561097 (ebook) | ISBN 9781629561103 (enhanced ebook)
Subjects: LCSH: Organizational learning. | Organizational change. | Organizational effectiveness. | Performance.
Classification: LCC HD58.82 .A53 2016 | DDC 650.1—dc23
LC record available at http://lccn.loc.gov/2015038239

You *are* the kindest, bravest, truest man I know

CONTENTS

CHAPTER 1

The New Need to Learn—and Our Mixed Response

My client was clearly not happy.

"I can't get my folks to think beyond what they're doing now!" he said, exasperated. At my inquiring look, he continued, "I asked everyone on my senior team to come up with one big new idea—something they thought could really move the business forward. And most of them just repeated back to me some variation of their existing goals. I don't know what to do to get them thinking differently."

A year into his new job as CEO of a media company just coming out of bankruptcy, he had already made sweeping changes: he completely revamped the senior team, spun off an underperforming division, and invested in a small part of the business where he saw future potential. His big frustration? Figuring out how to get his folks to follow him into the unknown, to be willing to experiment, to try new things.

"I imagine they're worried about being bad—and having you see them as bad," I replied.

He seemed puzzled.

"These people are good at their jobs," I went on, "and they believe you've hired them or kept them on because they're good at their jobs. They feel highly competent, even expert, and that makes them confident and comfortable—especially in this organization that's undergoing so much change." I leaned forward. "And now you're asking them to learn brand-new ways of operating, to suggest things they've never tried, to, perhaps, fail publicly. You're asking them—these middle-aged experts—to risk going back to being novices... to look dumb, to make mistakes, to not know how to do things. And it's enormously uncomfortable for them. They're resisting it by focusing on what they know they're good at and what they feel comfortable doing."

His face cleared. This particular executive, unlike most people, is okay with the discomfort of trying new things in public. Making mistakes and having to ask I-don't-know-what-that-means kinds of questions usually doesn't bother him much.

"So I need to encourage them to get comfortable with being uncomfortable," he said, starting to smile.

"Exactly," I said. "You need to let them know that not having everything perfectly mapped out is okay, and that you *expect* that some of their new ideas won't work. Most importantly, they have to know that you truly see trial and error as an inevitable part of breaking new ground. It's your responsibility to support them in becoming as comfortable as possible with the terribly awkward reality of exploring and understanding new ideas and new skills. You have to know—and let them know that you know—that to get good at anything that's new to you, you have to be willing to be bad at it first."

And thus the title of this book. You may get tired of me saying this over and over again, but it's the core of what we'll be talking and thinking about throughout this book, and it's a surprisingly unrecognized aspect of modern life. Because each one of us today is faced, moment to moment, with an overwhelming flood of information and possibilities that are brand new to us, we have to learn to be okay with being continuously uncomfortable in a way that no one in previous generations has had to do. As my client so wisely said it, we have to learn to be "comfortable with being uncomfortable."

Before You Decide This Is Another Book About Failure

I feel compelled to take a pause and do a bit of mind reading here. I believe you may, right at this moment, be thinking, *Oh, yeah—failing forward, failing fast. That's what she's talking about; I know about that. I've read books about failure…*

I believe you may be thinking something like that because it's how a pretty high percentage of people respond when we start talking to them about being bad first. The concept of "failing forward"—the title of John Maxwell's enormously popular book about how to respond well to failure—is an important one, and has helped a great many people accept their failures and mistakes rather than being overwhelmed or defeated by them.

So just to clarify: this is not a book about forging ahead through failure, or about how it takes a hundred bad ideas (failures) to come up with a good one, or about "grit" or resilience in the face of failure. What I'll be doing with you here is supporting you in building a few key habits of mind and action—mental skills that will allow you to acquire new capabilities quickly and continuously. This is an essential ability in today's world.

One of those mental skills—often the most difficult to develop—is the ability to accept the discomfort and disequilibrium that is an inevitable part of learning something new. Sometimes that involves accepting failure, but more often it simply means learning to be okay with slowness, awkwardness, not being clear about things, having to ask embarrassing questions—that is, learning to be okay with being bad first on the way to getting good. Interestingly, learning to be bad first (along with the other three mental skills I'll share with you throughout this book), can actually make it *less* likely that you'll fail massively during the learning process. But more about that later (in chapter 8). The important thing for our purposes here is that the ability to be bad first, along with the other mental skills you'll learn, is necessary to being a world-class learner, which is key to our success here in the twenty-first century.

Why Being Bad First Is So Essential Now

Let's talk a bit more about why this is so. Unless you're living somewhere deep in the equatorial rain forest or on top of a mountain, you know that we're living in an era of unprecedented change, driven largely by the enormous daily proliferation of new knowledge. One fascinating way to conceptualize the viral growth of human knowledge was posited in the early 1980s by futurist Buckminster Fuller. In his book *The Critical Path*, he established a concept he called the "knowledge-doubling curve." He started by assuming that all of humankind's collective knowledge in the year AD 1 was equal to one "knowledge unit." Fuller estimated that it then took until about AD 1500 for that cumulative human knowledge to double—for us to have discovered and understood, as a species, twice as much: at that point we had two "knowledge units."

He went on to propose that the next doubling—from two to four units—happened by 1750. He suggested that this second doubling was significantly accelerated by the invention of the printing press and the building of ocean-going ships that could travel fairly reliably from region to region, both of these innovations serving as powerful knowledge-spreading mechanisms.

He further estimated that our human knowledge had doubled again by around 1900. So, according to Fuller's theory, at this point—nineteen hundred years from the beginning of his knowledge-doubling curve—we humans had acquired or created eight "knowledge units." Pretty good work on the part of human-ity . . . but we were just getting started. At this point, the curve really started to accelerate.

Fuller proposed that the next doubling occurred around 1950, the next in the mid-70s, and the next in the late 1980s. And the acceleration continues: today, researchers estimate that human knowledge is doubling every twelve months—and some project that within the decade, it could be doubling *every twelve hours.*

Let's take a minute and put that into individual human terms. My mom's dad was born in 1887, right around the third doubling, when Fuller's model assumes human knowledge had increased to 800 percent of what it had been in the year AD 1. But by the time my children—his great-grandchildren—were born in the 1980s . . . *human knowledge had already increased again by 800 percent from when he was born.* You're reading that correctly: our knowledge had expanded as much during that one-hundred-year period as it had during the preceding nineteen hundred years.

I imagine you now have an image in your head of a geomet-ric curve: a line that starts out almost horizontal, gradually moves upward, starts to curve, and then heads suddenly north, almost exploding off the top of the chart. In terms of our knowledge as a race, we're now in that rocketing-upward part of the curve. But what does that mean for us, day to day? More than anything else, it means we have more options: this ramping up of knowledge has brought a concurrent ramping up of choices. Because we know so much more and understand so much more about ourselves and about the world around us, we all have many, many more choices to make at every moment than did our grandparents and great-grandparents—choices about what to focus on, what to learn, and how to use what we learn.

Here's an example. My mom, who was born in 1922, used to tell us how she and her dad constructed a crystal radio set so they could listen to the account of Charles Lindbergh's solo flight from New York to Paris in May of 1927—the first time anyone had crossed the Atlantic alone in an airplane. She remembered her dad telling her that Lindbergh was the first person in history to be in New York one day and in Paris the next. Nearly everyone in the world who had access to information about Lindbergh's flight was focused on that event, from the hundreds of people who were there when he landed in an airfield outside Paris, to the thousands who were able to listen in, thanks to the modern miracle of radio, or who were informed through the telegrams and phone calls that sped around the world, to the millions who read about it over the following days in their local newspapers. For weeks after it happened, it was likely the most important event on most people's minds. It probably took a number of months for the news of his success to get to everyone in the world who was interested in hearing it.

Contrast that with today: any event of any importance (and lots that we'd argue aren't that important at all) zips from one side of the world to the other in mere moments. From presidential elections to the events of the Arab Spring, from government scandals to celebrity babies, from groundbreaking medical discoveries to scary pandemics: we have access to any and all information in the blink of an eye, and we have to decide, moment to moment, how to think about it, how to respond to it, and whether it affects our lives.

And this explosion of information (with its resulting explosion of choices about where to put our attention) has also created secondary explosions—in our scientific and technological knowledge, for instance, and in our beliefs and expectations about society and individual rights. Anyone from the early twentieth century magically transported into the twenty-first would be overwhelmed by the differences in daily life since his time, on both a technological and a cultural level. Cars are a part of every family's daily life; pocket devices make phone calls, take pictures, and hold all our information; airplanes, television, antibiotics, and computers are facts of everyday life; the status of women and people of color has changed dramatically; and a much wider variety of lifestyles, religions, and philosophies are accepted as legitimate and commonplace.

But what does this have to do with my original point, that here in the twenty-first century it's essential for us to learn how to "be bad first"? This explosion of knowledge, and the technological, scientific, and cultural advances that have resulted, have also dramatically changed how we learn and how we work—and what it takes to succeed at work and in our lives.

For someone growing up in the early part of the twentieth century, the expectations around learning were fairly clear: you would go to school to learn the basics, then land a job and learn what you needed in order to do that job reasonably well. You would go on to work in some version of that job until you retired. This was true whether you were a doctor or a pipe fitter: the vast majority of people learned a trade or profession, and practiced it throughout their working lives. Of course, some people aspired to be excellent at their chosen profession, and those people might take pride in learning the new techniques and approaches that occasionally arose, or in figuring out a better way to do some essential part of the job. But for the most part, someone who started working in 1925 would most likely be engaged in very much the same kind of work when he or she (usually he) retired with a gold watch in 1965.

In that environment, the ability to learn new things quickly and continuously wasn't that important. People assumed, for the most part, that the bulk of learning would happen early in their lives, and that by the time they got to be adults, they could relax into being competent (or even excellent), and just make the effort necessary to maintain their existing skills and knowledge. Changing jobs—let alone changing careers—was seen for the most part as somewhat suspect, a sign of low commitment, poor work habits, or an inability to get along with people. Those old movies from the '30s and '40s, where someone says, "he's a reporter" or "she's a teacher"—that was an accurate reflection of the way people thought of themselves and one another: you had a job, and you were identified with that job until you retired from it, and, in fact, probably until you died.

Fast-forward to today, when most people coming into the workforce expect that they will have a variety of jobs and work at a number of companies, perhaps with a stint or two of working freelance mixed in—or even spend part of their career creating and working in their own company. The geometric increase of human knowledge has made it inevitable that nearly every job has changed and will change dramatically over the course of any person's work life. And our new relationship with choice—that daily, hourly choice has become the norm, and that we will be making different choices about the same topic as new possibilities emerge—has made it acceptable for us to choose different work at different times in our lives.

Three Generations: As Change Accelerates

This sea change in our careers and what we expect of them, driven by the geometric increase in knowledge over the past three generations, has affected most of us directly: we see it written in the family histories of almost everyone we know. Your grandparents approached work differently than did your parents; their approach differs from yours, and yours from that of your children.

My own family is no exception. My dad was born in Valley, Nebraska, in 1921, and grew up wanting to be a lawyer. After Pearl Harbor, he left college to join the Coast Guard, and fought in the Pacific theater of World War II for three years. After the war, he came home to marry my mom, his college sweetheart, and attend law school at the University of Nebraska on the GI Bill. After he graduated and passed the bar, they settled in Omaha, where he joined my grandfather's law practice. They raised four kids and were active in the community. My dad practiced labor law in Omaha his whole life, until his death in 1988. He never expected to change careers, or to leave Omaha, and would have been puzzled at the idea. Why leave a career he loved and was good at, in a town where he had settled, where his kids had gown up, and where he had been successful both as an involved citizen and in his chosen profession? He didn't have to think about doing anything differently: the reasonable pace of change in those decades allowed him to live his life in much the same way throughout that forty-year period.

Though he was an intelligent and thoughtful guy, I can't imagine him taking time to seriously question the idea that his path was pretty much what a career was supposed to be: you found something you liked and were good at, and you worked at it to support your family for the rest of your working life. End of story.

I remember my mom and dad talking in worried voices about my uncle, a salesman who had had to change companies and move to new cities a few times in his career. It wasn't that he was in danger of not being able to support his family, it was simply a cause for concern that he hadn't been able to stay with one company throughout his career.

My siblings and I, born in the next generation, took far more divergent paths—which we also thought perfectly acceptable, given the accelerating pace of change in our young adult years. Of the four of us, only my older sister has had a single career—she's a college professor—and even she has lived in three different cities since college, has taught at two different universities, and did her graduate work at yet a third. My two brothers and I all chose a kind of career path that must have seemed exceedingly strange to our Depression-era parents, but was very common among baby boomers: we spent our twenties and early thirties *creating* careers for ourselves, that is, inventing new work rather than slipping into existing jobs. It was our way of taking best advantage of the possibilities we saw before us—responding to the explosion of new knowledge and new technology around us in the '70s and '80s. My older brother created a business renovating and brokering high-end pianos and is a nationally respected piano technician and teacher of other technicians; my younger brother is a well-known journalist, social commentator, and best-selling novelist; I'm an author and the founding partner of Proteus, a consulting company that focuses on leader readiness. However, we didn't entirely abandon the find-something-and-stick-with-it credo of our parents' generation. We've each been doing some version of those careers we invented for decades now: we baby boomers, for the most part, still believed that the smart thing to do was find a good career and commit to it.

My children and my siblings' children, however, have moved even further away from the "one career" credo, as the knowledge curve has really started to shoot up. Most of them are millennials, and each has had a number of jobs. Some of them have already explored more than one profession. For example, my older daughter graduated from college with a degree in marketing communications and worked in PR and customer service for a few years. She realized it wasn't as satisfying and interesting to her as she'd hoped, so she went back to school and got a master's degree in early childhood education, and is now teaching in a progressive independent school. Though she loves teaching, and is glad she made the change, she doesn't take for granted that she'll be a teacher for the rest of her career. She's learning and adjusting as she goes, assuming that the main skill she'll need is the ability to adapt to changing circumstances as she looks to craft career paths that she'll enjoy and that will allow her to grow with and support her husband and children.

She and her generational counterparts rarely define themselves by their careers; they see career as something that will change as they change, in response to changing needs and circumstances. One study shows that these millennials expect to have fifteen to twenty different jobs by the time they retire. Not just promotions into a slightly bigger or more senior version of their current job, mind you—fifteen to twenty entirely different jobs. In fact, most people now in their twenties and thirties don't assume that the job they have today will even exist forty years from now, let alone that they'll have anything resembling that job by the time they retire. If they retire at all: 50 percent of millennials don't expect to have access to Social Security or corporate retirement plans when they hit retirement age, and almost that many say they want to find work that's so meaningful to them that they may not ever want to retire completely.

This same shift—from stability to fluidity—has happened on an organizational level. In the early twentieth century, the business landscape was dominated by big companies we all assumed would last forever. (Remember TWA? General Foods? Arthur Andersen?) Now, many of the companies that immediately come to mind when we think of successful enterprises are those that have arisen out of new technologies spawned by new knowledge (Amazon, Google, Apple, Samsung). And even the largest companies seem vulnerable these days to the sweeping changes in technology and consumer behavior driven by this ramping up of knowledge. For example, on a *Wikipedia* list of the world's largest companies by revenue, almost one-third are in the oil and gas industry. What will happen to these mega-companies as our knowledge of alternative fuels and their profitable application increases exponentially?

Just like the rest of us, the folks who run these companies will have to learn and change—or fail. In the words of Arie de Geus, a wonderfully agile thinker and for many years the head of strategy for Royal Dutch Shell (interestingly, number two on that list of the world's largest companies by revenue), "The ability to learn faster than your competitors may be the only sustainable competitive advantage."[1]

Let's focus on the one element of our world that is making that statement more and more true every day.

More Knowledge = More Communication = More Knowledge

We've been talking about the proliferation of knowledge and options over the past century, and the technological explosion spawned by that new knowledge. But we haven't yet talked directly about the Internet, the twenty-first century's most powerful knowledge distribution mechanism, even more potent than the printing press and seagoing vessels in terms of its ability to accelerate the advance of human knowledge. The advent of the Internet as a means of communicating and expanding our knowledge base makes "learning faster than your competitors" both more possible and more necessary.

If it's true that human knowledge will be doubling every year by the end of this decade, we have the Internet to thank. For example, every scientific or medical breakthrough that happens today is immediately available online all over the world in complete detail, so that researchers can access that new knowledge instantly, and begin to build upon it. The same is true of business innovation: in the old days (say, 1980), when people started a truly new kind of business, they could assume that they would have a couple of years to get their feet under them before they'd have much competition. No more. New ventures can succeed almost overnight, given the fact that social media can be harnessed to spread the word about their services or products with minimal investment. But the same viral-ness of communication that allows for that success also makes that success completely and thoroughly visible to potential competitors, who can start replicating those approaches and products the next day.

Given all this, it seems clear that those who succeed in today's world will be those who can acquire and apply new knowledge and new skills quickly and continuously. That's really the premise of this book: that at this point in history, where knowledge is increasing exponentially, where work is changing daily, where advancements in every area of discipline nearly outpace our ability to communicate them—*the ability to learn well and quickly is the most important skill we can have.*

And that requires, among a number of things that we'll talk about throughout this book, being willing to be a novice over and over again—being willing to be bad at things on the way to getting good at them. There's no way around it, I'm afraid: in order to thrive in this new world, you have to let go—on a daily basis—of the idea that to be an adult means to be an expert. You have to stop thinking that your primary goal at work and in life is to tick all the boxes correctly and not make any mistakes. That belief will be reassuring in the moment, but over time it will land you in the dustbin of history.

But Not Knowing Things Feels So...Bad

We may realize intellectually that being successful these days requires being open to continuous, disruptive learning, but that doesn't mean we like it...or that we're very good at it. The *Financial Times* noted in a recent article, for instance, that corporate learning tends to be largely ineffective. "Companies' spending on training and development accounts for hundreds of billion pounds globally each year. But every year, according to successive empirical studies, only 5 to 20 per cent of what is learnt finds its way back into the workplace."[2]

Somehow, our attempts to teach and learn new and needed skills and understanding at work aren't working very well.

This may be at least partly because our efforts at supporting people to acquire new skills and knowledge don't take into account that we so often resist learning new things—especially when those things are different from what we already know, or when we have to take on new ways of behaving or thinking in order to learn them. A study completed in 2010 at Cornell University by researchers Jennifer Mueller, Shimul Melwani, and Jack Goncalo focused on our conflicted relationship with new ideas.[3]

They used a test to determine people's implicit attitudes toward new ideas. The test offered a list of words that described new or untested things (for instance, *novel, creative, inventive, original*) and other words that described standard or known things (such as *practical, functional, constructive,* and *useful*), and asked the study participants to categorize each word as "good" or "bad." The study found that although people *say* that they like and want creativity and newness, when it came to categorizing the words that describe familiar things and unfamiliar things, they saw the "familiar" words as more positive and the "new" words as less positive, time and time again.

No matter what we assert about wanting to be creative and being open to new ideas, we tend to have a harder time accepting and feeling positive toward new ideas than toward those already proven and understood. One finding from the study was that people may believe they are open to insights and innovations but are generally only receptive to new ideas that fit with existing practices and maintain predictability.

In other words, we like new ideas or new skills as long as they reinforce our existing beliefs and experience. As I said early on in this chapter, we really like being good at things and feeling as though we're competent. So if new knowledge comfortably supports and expands our sense of ourselves as expert, we're fans of it. However, if the new knowledge makes us question what we know, or feel like we're not as expert as we thought (and have told everybody that we were), we resist it.

In the late nineties, a British scholar named James Atherton demonstrated very poignantly that, though we say we want to learn and take in new ideas, when those new ideas start to poke holes in what we know, or send us into realms where we feel like novices—i.e., clumsy and inexpert—we often close down and resist that learning. Atherton notes, "Resistance to learning is a phenomenon well-known to most tutors and trainers of adults, but has received remarkably little attention in the literature."[4]

By way of exploring this resistance, Atherton set up an interview-based study of social services professionals taking in-service training programs. This wasn't some wacky adventure in free-form learning: it was knowledge the participants needed in order to succeed in their careers, and for the most part, the participants were not overtly negative toward either being required to attend the training or the need to acquire this new knowledge—they saw why the training was necessary and were reasonably open to taking it.

However, when Atherton and his colleagues began investigating the participants' *actual* responses to the training, they found something very different. When confronted with new facts and knowledge, especially knowledge that seemed to contradict what they already knew, they often simply shut down. Study participants became confused, unable to concentrate, even angry when asked to learn things that would cause them to operate in new ways or rethink current practices. A number of participants "reported… a largely inexplicable inability to listen to or to understand ideas which they themselves felt they should have been able to manage intellectually with no difficulty. They used phrases like 'I just couldn't get my head round it.'"[5]

I've seen this for years in the executives we coach. If we're working to help someone improve in an area where that person already has some competence—is okay at delegating, for instance, but needs to get better—that's usually relatively easy. Especially if the delegation model we're teaching aligns pretty well with what she has already been doing. But if an executive is really poor at delegating (and particularly if that person sees himself as an "expert" leader), it can be very tough. We often get the same kind of confusion, irritation, and inability to grasp relatively straightforward ideas or change fairly simple behaviors that Atherton encountered in his study. It can take a good deal of time, care, and attention to help executives adopt the mindset that will allow them to learn new skills necessary to their success.

In short, we don't like being thrown into that "be bad first" position; as adults, we simply don't like to do what feels like going backward, to being novices all over again. We secretly hope that we've left behind forever that feeling of incompetence that we have when we're confronted with new knowledge or skills. We want to be fully competent adults who have it all together. As adults, having to start from scratch to learn something brand new can be confusing, demoralizing, even downright scary.

Like the executives in the example I gave at the beginning of the chapter—who may have verbally supported their boss's focus on innovation, and may even have intellectually understood how important it was for them to open up to new ideas and new ways of doing things—when it came to the point of actually needing to step out of their comfort zone and do it, Atherton's study participants shut down. It felt too uncomfortable, too professionally and personally vulnerable, to venture into that vast territory of "I don't know this." They retreated to the known, turning their backs on the possibility of learning those new ways of understanding and operating that might carry them and their company forward into a more successful future.

So, here in this moment, when knowledge and the possibilities that arise from that knowledge are expanding exponentially—even as we speak—a key question for each of us is: How can we overcome our hesitation and our resistance to new learning, in order to become those "masters of mastery" who will best succeed in the twenty-first century?

The good news is, we've all got something inside of us that will help. We may hate to be bad at things—but we love getting good at things.

CHAPTER 2

The Drive to Mastery:
We Want to Get Good

suspect you've understood by now that I want you to be keenly aware of two things: how critical it is for you to become a skilled and fluent acquirer of new knowledge and skills in order to succeed in this century, and how deeply we can each resist the necessary "novice" state that accompanies any truly new learning. However, I don't want to you to be overly demoralized by this, because there are some qualities built into us humans that help to make these truths less daunting. The most important one: we may hate being bad at things, but we *love* to get good at them.

The *Angry Birds* phenomenon is a great example. I first heard about *Angry Birds* from a client whose preteen daughters had introduced it to him a few months earlier. "I can't stop playing it," he said. "It's the craziest thing." At my skeptical look, he continued, "Just try it, you'll see."

Curious, I downloaded it onto my iPhone that night, and started to explore the world of wingless birds with strange powers and their archenemies, an army of thieving pigs living in fantastically ramshackle palaces. The next time I looked at my watch, I'd attained my first three-star score—and sixty minutes had magically disappeared.

Unless you've been living under a rock since 2010, you're probably aware that *Angry Birds* is one of the most downloaded "freemium" games of all time, with more than two billion downloads worldwide. Anyone who spends time on subways, in airports, or riding commuter trains can attest not only to the popularity of the game but to the single-minded concentration it engenders in its fans.

Over the past few years, the passion for *Angry Birds* has begun to morph into an equally mad passion for *Candy Crush* and all its knockoffs, and I'm sure there's another game being developed at this moment that will suck us in to the same extent.

What's the attraction of these simple games? Why are otherwise responsible people willing to waste hours and hours killing pigs and crushing candy? For one thing, *Angry Birds* and similar games are drop-dead easy to learn. Despite its unprecedented popularity, you notice that no one has hung out a shingle as an *Angry Birds* tutor (in fact, if you search "learning Angry Birds," you get websites about how to create online games, and websites that use *Angry Birds* as a framework for teaching other things). My four-year-old granddaughter has already figured it out.

And since you can learn it by yourself and get some positive results very quickly (you're killing pigs within the first few minutes), the "being bad first" phase is both short and painless. In fact, you can mess up over and over while you try various strategies without incurring any of the negative outcomes that usually arise from "being bad" at something—nobody else is observing your ineptitude, and there are no material consequences...you simply hit the reset button and everything is instantly just as it was before your last entirely unsuccessful pig-slaying attempt.

The fact that learning the game takes an end run around our built-in "novice-ness resistors" explains how so many millions of us have gotten pulled into playing *Angry Birds*...but what keeps us going?

Two researchers at the University of Rochester, Edward Deci and Richard Ryan, introduced a broad theory of human motivation they called *self-determination theory* in the 1980s. Hundreds of other researchers and practitioners have since explored and refined it, by far the most well-known being Daniel Pink in his best-selling book *Drive: The Surprising Truth About What Motivates Us.* Deci and Ryan discovered that the most widespread motivations for human behavior, regardless of gender, culture, or age, are three drives they named competence, self-determination, and connectedness, which Pink reframed as *mastery, autonomy,* and *purpose.* We deeply long to have the freedom (autonomy) to get good at things (mastery) that are meaningful to us (purpose).

While we'd be hard pressed to argue that *Angry Birds* offers much in the way of "purpose" or deeper meaning, it certainly gets high marks for autonomy and, most especially, *mastery.* It's possible to get almost infinitely better at it. When I (still) play, I focus on trying to get three-star scores without using any special tools. My husband operates at a more expert level, refusing to leave a screen until he's demolished all its pigs with a single bird. After that, I suspect, comes the rarified goal of getting all the pigs with a single bird on the first try. And so on.

And that, I believe, explains the ongoing popularity of *Angry Birds*—and of other similar games as well: *we love to get good at things.* Mastery, as Deci and Ryan discovered more than thirty years ago, is intrinsically motivating to us.

Mastery Makes Us Feel Good

Researchers over the past decade have devoted a great deal of thought to investigating the connection between mastery and personal satisfaction. Andrew Przybylski, a social scientist based at the University of Oxford, has done extensive research about what makes electronic games and social media motivating to people. About ten years ago, he conducted a series of experiments with two colleagues to find out the effects of feeling competent—that is, achieving mastery—on people playing video games.[1]

The participants played *Super Mario* for twenty minutes; they were asked a series of questions both before and after playing to determine their self-perceived levels of competence (mastery) and autonomy, and also to find out how they might behave differently as a result of feeling more or less competent or autonomous. As expected, Przybylski and his collaborators found that those who felt more competent at the end of the play session—those who felt that they had come closer to mastering the game—wanted to keep playing. This isn't so surprising; a pillar of self-determination theory, as noted above, is that we're deeply motivated to get good at things, and generally, when we feel we're good at something, we want to keep doing it.

However, they also found a strong correlation between the feeling of competence and participants' overall sense of well-being; the researchers discovered that "mood, vitality, and self-esteem" were higher in those who felt competent. In other words, we not only feel good about mastering new skills—mastering new skills makes us feel good about ourselves.

Mastery and Survival

If you reflect upon our history as a race, it makes sense that mastering new skills should be so gratifying. Imagine a prehistoric tribe, fighting to survive in a world of climactic extremes, large predators, and inconsistent food sources. Those ancient humans who got good at the most critical tasks—making fires, avoiding being eaten, finding food, and protecting themselves from the elements—were more likely to survive and reproduce. This argues that the human urge toward mastery isn't just a modern feel-good innovation: it's a survival instinct. In other words, the will toward mastery has been bred into us over thousands of generations. Throughout history, those who were best at mastering the skills needed to stay alive managed to stay alive. And those folks were then able to pass on that trait, their will toward mastery, to succeeding generations.

And, as with the other things we need to do in order to survive—eat, sleep, stay warm, procreate—mastery feels great. Those things most key to our continued existence are generally the things we find most attractive. No wonder mastery makes us feel so good.

I often see the power of this drive toward mastery in the professionals we train. Two or three times every year, two Proteus colleagues and I conduct a weeklong management and leadership development session for a group of sixty high-potential mid-level women managers from the cable industry. On an objective level, it's a bit grueling: they spend eight or nine hours, for five days straight, working on improving their skills in managing and leading people. They get lots of feedback—not all of it positive—and they spend the majority of their time learning and practicing skills that may be new to them, or in which they may need to make a good deal of improvement. There's a lot of being bad first going on. And yet, at the end of every session, almost all the participants, while very tired, are nearly giddy with joy and pride at their new levels of mastery, and are excited about going back to work and putting into practice all that they've learned.

Given how important it is, at this particular moment in human history, for each of us to become world-class, continuous masters of mastery, it's lucky for all of us that we're so strongly motivated to do so. It's a wonderful and necessary balancer to our resistance to being bad—and we'll talk about how to take best advantage of this deep will toward mastery in chapter 4.

Another Lucky Break

There's yet another piece of good fortune to go along with our love of mastery: we are all capable of continuing to master new knowledge and skills throughout our lives. This may sound obvious, but until fairly recently, scientists believed that this wasn't the case. They thought that once people were past early childhood, their ability to learn declined steeply. And this belief—that once you're an adult it's much more difficult to learn new things—wasn't just restricted to the laboratory. As a society, we have tended to believe that "you can't teach an old dog new tricks," and so we expect that adults will be less and less able to learn new skills or be open to new approaches the older they get. For example, you hear this theory offered as a rationale for the difficulty most adults have in learning a second language: that our brains, as adults, are simply not as "plastic" as those of children. (I'm convinced this is actually a "being bad first" problem, but more on this later.) You can also see this belief reflected in media coverage of older people's accomplishments: when someone over the age of sixty achieves any kind of knowledge breakthrough or becomes adept at a new profession, the stories about that person's accomplishments tend to focus not on the remarkable nature of the learning or the success itself, but on how surprising it is that the learning or success should have happened for someone of such an advanced age.

This belief about our ever-declining learning ability was based on three assumptions, widely shared by neurologists and brain researchers. These scientists thought, until very recently, that each baby had at birth all the brain cells he would ever have. They further believed that those brain cells would begin to die off almost immediately (and would continue to do so as the person aged). And, finally it was thought that the remaining brain cells would, over time, lose their "plasticity"—their ability to change structure and function in response to new experiences.

These assumptions imply that, from the moment of birth, we become continuously less able to learn new things, and there's nothing we can do about it. If these beliefs had been true, how could we possibly have responded to our twenty-first century imperative to be great learners?

Fortunately for all of us, it turns out that these three assumptions were dead wrong. (Thank goodness for today's ongoing explosion of knowledge in the sciences.) While it's true that we start losing brain cells as soon as we're born, we also keep *adding* new brain cells throughout our lives, and those cells work just as well for learning as the ones we had at the beginning of our lives, the ones we used to figure out how to walk and talk. As molecular biologist and brain scientist John Medina notes in his book *Brain Rules*, "Researchers have shown that some regions of the adult brain stay as malleable as a baby's brain, so we can grow new connections, strengthen existing connections, and even create new neurons, allowing all of us to be lifelong learners. [T]he adult brain . . . continues creating neurons within the regions normally involved in learning. These new neurons show the same plasticity as those of newborns."[2]

In other words, we can keep on learning—and learning well—until we die. That means that there's no neurological reason for us not to take up Sudoku at eighty or decide to learn a new language in our fifties, no reason we can't become as adept at using social media or growing a garden or running a business at sixty or ninety as we can at twenty or thirty.

I coach a CEO in his seventies who is a great example of this. A few years ago, his company needed a new head of marketing, so he was starting the search for a chief marketing officer. As he talked to me about it, I could tell that his understanding of what a CMO could and should do was quite limited. The previous marketing head had been there for many years, and had contented himself with fulfilling a fairly small and tactical marketing role: responding to requests for taglines and ads, tweaking the company logo for different uses, and creating premiums for conventions. My client had never experienced a great strategic marketer who could be a catalyst for thinking about the brand and communicating that brand to various audiences in a compelling way.

When I suggested to my client that he spend some time talking to a "modern CMO," so he could get a sense of what was possible, he didn't resist. He got curious (another key element of learning that we'll talk about at length in chapter 6). I connected him with a CMO who I knew would be enthusiastic, articulate, and patient in explaining the new science of marketing to him. They had a long, in-depth conversation; my friend also suggested other useful people and resources. At the end of a month of exploration, my client had a completely different understanding of the benefits a good marketer could provide to him and his organization. He rewrote the job description, changed the direction of his search, and ultimately found an excellent CMO who is helping his company to understand and market its brand much more effectively. I'm confident this CEO will keep using his brain's capability and his own drive toward mastery to keep growing and learning as long as he lives (which may be a very long time—in a conversation a few weeks ago he noted to me that, "on a bad day, I feel like I'm twenty-nine").

So What's the Problem?

The new research that confirms our ability to continue to learn throughout our lives is good news. We need desperately, at this point in our history, to be able to keep learning every day, to continue to become competent in new ways of operating and new ways of thinking throughout our lives. And, to our great good fortune, we are both mentally capable of doing that—our brains can grow and make new connections throughout our lives—and deeply attracted toward doing it—mastery is one of our strongest intrinsic motivations.

The problem is the one we discussed in the first chapter: we so much love being good at things that we really resist not being good at things. And this love of being competent, of feeling like an expert, can seriously impede our ability to be open to new learning.

And not being open to new and necessary learning can put a serious crimp in our ability to succeed in today's world. I have a friend and client who is one of the best media marketing executives I've ever known. He is extraordinarily gifted at understanding how to conceive of and speak about a brand so as to make it compelling for that brand's consumers and potential consumers. He's built a great career over the last thirty years by becoming increasingly good at doing this. He is also a talented presenter, so he's often asked to speak at conferences about his area of mastery. He shares with audiences how he gets into the mindset of consumers and builds brands that speak to them in ways that resonate for them.

Last year he and I were talking, and he told me that he had just had a big aha about his approach to marketing, one that he believed was both important to his success and difficult for him to accept. He shared with me that he has been resisting the movement in marketing over the past few years toward more reliance on data, toward making more use of the increasing amount and complexity of information available about consumers and their habits and preferences, and away from relying only on the honed consumer instincts that have made him and others like him successful. Until recently, he said, when people would start talking to him about the increasing importance of "big data" in marketing, he would pooh-pooh it, responding that, although it might be necessary for marketing big-ticket, single-sale, highly commoditized items like cars or condos, it didn't really apply to television programming.

But then, he said, he began to open up to the fact that he was *blinded by his expertise* (his phrase): that he felt so comfortable in his position of marketing guru that he was dismissing the importance of data-based marketing because it meant he'd have to start from scratch in learning this new approach. Now he's deeply immersed in figuring out how to build this new expertise, and how it will relate to or negate his preexisting skills and knowledge. But my friend is a very self-aware and unusually open guy: I suspect many experts of his caliber would have clung to their outmoded expertise for much longer—and done damage both to their current job and their career prospects.

History is rife with examples of attachment to existing expertise operating as a barrier that closes people off to new learning, from the Catholic Church's denunciation of Galileo for asserting that the sun was the center of the solar system to doctors in the nineteenth century laughing at the idea that their unwashed hands could be causing childbed fever to the infamous 1977 quote from computer industry executive Ken Olsen: "There is no reason for any individual to have a computer in his home."

Going from Master to Novice— Over and Over

And there you have the shape of the problem. We love being good at stuff, and we're capable of getting good at stuff whether we're one or one hundred. But we really, really don't like having to go back to being a novice after we've become an expert at some things. We'd much rather simply continue to rely upon, identify with, and get better at the things we're already good at doing.

But as my marketing friend is discovering, that just won't work. No matter what you're good at now, if you hold on to how your area of expertise looked and worked five years ago, or five minutes ago, you'll get left behind.

We each have to be willing and able to start over again and again, to be comfortable—or at least comfortable enough—with going back to being a novice.

And it is possible; there are people who are doing it. Consider

Norman Lear. He has been a remarkable learner and "explorer of the new" for more than seven decades. I've had a the good fortune to work with Norman in his company, Act III Communications, and in People for the American Way, the civil liberties advocacy organization he founded in the early 1980s.

Norman's first career, begun after WWII, was in public relations, but after just a few years he moved with his family to California and there discovered the new medium of television. Within a few years he was writing for TV full time, and he went on to write some of the best-known and most highly rated comedies in television history, among them *All in the Family, Sanford and Son, Maude,* and *The Jeffersons.* By the late sixties, Lear had evolved into what he considers the "second act" of his media career: producing and directing films. In fact, in 1974, he and a partner started a production company called T.A.T. Communications Company—the "T.A.T." stood for "tuchus affen tisch," a Yiddish phrase meaning roughly "to put your butt on the line." Which, by the way, they did time and time again, trying out new genres and new ways of filming old genres that resonated with audiences worldwide. For example, Lear is credited with giving Rob Reiner his start as a director by funding and producing Reiner's rock "mockumentary" *This Is Spinal Tap.* Reiner and his cocreators couldn't find anyone who understood what they were trying to do with the film until Lear stepped in and saved the day. He told me many years later, "None of them really knew what they were doing—and I certainly didn't—but it just seemed like such a wonderful idea."

Then, in 1986, Lear founded Act III Communications. He described it to me as the "third act" of his career, where he could experiment with bringing together the various aspects of media to see what emerged from the combination. To date, these elements have included Act III Theatres, Broadcasting, and Publishing, as well as Concord Music Group and Village Roadshow Pictures.

In addition to breaking new ground in TV and films, Lear has also supported first amendment rights and various liberal political causes over the past sixty years, earning both censure (he was on Richard Nixon's "enemies list") and praise (he was awarded the National Medal of Arts in 1999).

Lear published his autobiography, *Even This I Get to Experience,* in October of 2014, at the age of ninety-two. In the book, he notes, "In my ninety-plus years, I've lived a multitude of lives." And my observation, in listening to and working with him, is that he has approached each of these lives with joy and excitement rather than the resistance and unhappiness most of us demonstrate when we have to move out of our expert comfort zone.

Norman Lear, and others like him, are masters of mastery, who have somehow figured out how to face every learning challenge by setting down their expertise and being willing and able to start fresh, to learn anew. I've learned, from him and from thousands of other clients and colleagues over the years, how we can continuously overcome our own resistance to new learning and take best advantage of our deeply ingrained human will to improve. These people have cracked the code of learning, and now I want to help you crack that code as well. We're about to embark on a simple path to mastery, you and I, called ANEW.

CHAPTER 3

Cracking the Code: Michelangelo and ANEW

Let's start by looking at one of history's most skilled masters of mastery. We'll travel back in time, to early 1507, in Rome:

Michelangelo could put it off no longer. For two years he had been able to evade Pope Julius II's insistence that he paint the ceiling of the Sistine Chapel, but only because the pope was focusing most of his energy on delicate and far-reaching efforts to bring accord among the emerging nation-states of Europe. Michelangelo, relieved, had worked on other commissions with which he felt more comfortable, while sending a stream of letters to the pope telling him why the timing wasn't right to start working on the Sistine ceiling. But now the pope had returned to Rome, victorious from a decisive wrangle with the French. Within days of his triumphant reentry into the city, Julius met with Michelangelo and demanded that he begin work on the ceiling immediately.

The artist had been resisting the pope's commission for a number of reasons. First, he considered himself primarily a sculptor rather than a painter, and didn't want to spend years on a gigantic project that he didn't feel he was best suited to complete. He also didn't like the pope's design for the ceiling (and that's a hard thing to say to a pope). Finally, he knew that, should he take the job, it would involve years of uncomfortable, painstaking labor.

But once he realized there was no avoiding Pope Julius's "request," Michelangelo began to figure out how to make the best of it. First he negotiated for and finally received permission to create a much more intricate and grand design than the one envisioned by the pope. Next, he became engrossed in solving the purely technical problems presented by the task: how to adapt the techniques of fresco (painting with a colored wash on damp plaster) to a gigantic space (133 by 46 feet), while suspended almost 70 feet from the ground.

By the time Michelangelo had permission to, in his words, "do as he liked" in terms of the design, and had created what he believed were viable solutions for the technical problems presented by the project, his attitude had changed dramatically—he told friends he could hardly wait to get started. In May of 1508, the thirty-three-year-old artist signed a contract with the Vatican and began work on what many consider the single greatest work of art in Western history.

Because he had never worked in fresco as a mature artist, but only as an apprentice in the studio of his master Ghirlandaio, Michelangelo hired assistants, many from his old master's studio, who had more experience with the medium. They helped him figure out how to apply the technique to the massive dimensions of the ceiling, and how to work on a painting surface that was arched above them.

When it came to solving the problem of creating a

physical structure to support him and his assistants, however, Michelangelo had to rely on his own ingenuity. When he realized that scaffoldings built up from the floor would be both hugely expensive and dangerously unstable, he started to wonder how else he could get his crew up near the ceiling in a way that was reasonably stable and safe. In following his curiosity, he ended up designing an innovative scaffolding structure that consisted of a moveable platform resting on brackets inserted into purpose-made holes in the walls, holes that could be filled in after the work was completed.

The work went slowly at first, both because Michelangelo was inexperienced with the medium and because the unusual size and configuration of the surface created unique problems. For example, he discovered about a third of the way through the project that the need to keep such large areas moist enough to paint meant the plaster would often get moldy before it dried. He ripped out huge areas of the work that had been damaged by mold, and asked one of his assistants, Jacopo Torni, known as L'Indaco, an experienced fresco painter, for a solution. L'Indaco created a more mold-resistant plaster formula, which Michelangelo used for the remainder of the job (and which, in fact, subsequently became the standard for Italian fresco painting).

By the end of the four years it took to complete the project, Michelangelo felt himself an accomplished fresco painter. However, he noted, "If people knew how hard I worked to get my mastery, it wouldn't seem so wonderful at all." Michelangelo's astonishing work contains 343 figures, mostly life sized, and tells the entire creation story as recounted in the Bible. It also includes all the prophets who foretold Jesus's birth, as well as a roster of Jesus's ancestors and a host of angelic creatures large and small. Five hundred years later, more than five million visitors a year marvel at this creation of a single man who made every effort at the beginning to avoid the project altogether, telling the pope "painting is not my art—I cannot succeed."

What Does This Have to Do with Us Now?

Before I deconstruct Michelangelo's approach to learning, let me answer a question I suspect you may have at this point. You might be wondering why I've chosen to use Michelangelo—dead for more than four hundred years—as someone who exemplifies the skills of mastery we need in order to succeed in the twenty-first century. Here's how I see it: Michelangelo's challenge in painting the Sistine Chapel ceiling was not dissimilar to a challenge each of us faces every day, that is: *How can I learn to do new things quickly and well—especially things I've never done before and am not even sure how to go about learning?*

Clearly, Michelangelo was the kind of power learner that each of us needs to become in order to succeed in today's world. In fact, one of his favorite sayings, which he employed throughout his life as a response to compliments on his work, was *Ancora imparo*—"I am still learning." His experience in painting the Sistine Chapel ceiling provides us with a wonderful example of the mental skills that are key to this kind of high-payoff learning.

Because a lot of what I do for a living boils down to supporting people in learning new skills and capabilities—whether through providing executive coaching, designing leadership and management training, or writing business books—I've thought a great deal, over the past three decades, about how we learn and how we get in the way of our own learning. Along the way, I've noticed certain people throughout history—Michelangelo, da Vinci, Galileo, Christine de Pisan, Albert Einstein, George Washington Carver, Marie Curie, Steve Jobs, and Norman Lear, to name a few—who have been unusually good at learning new things and applying that knowledge to break new ground and create success for themselves and others. I've reflected on how each of them approached learning (to the extent I knew or could find out about it), and I've also observed hundreds of coaching clients and thousands of training clients, and noticed what they did either to support their own learning or to impede it.

Then, a few years ago, I wrote a book called *Leading So People Will Follow*. It outlines the core traits that followers look for in a leader before they'll fully sign up for that person's leadership, and explains how to develop those traits in order to become a more followable leader. When the book came out, I did lots of interviews about it, and the one question that interviewers invariably asked was, "Do you think good leaders are born or made?" I could tell that most interviewers believed they already knew the answer to the question; they thought that good leaders are born that way. Most people believe that, I've found: that you're either a good leader or not—like having blue eyes or brown eyes—and there's not much you can do about it.

I would always answer the question in the same way: that I see natural leadership capability as existing along a bell curve, with some people at the top of the curve who are simply, for whatever reason, natively skilled leaders, and people at the bottom of the curve who have very little innate leadership capability and probably should pursue a career that doesn't require them to lead others. I would then add that I see most of us residing in that broad middle of the curve, having somewhere from a moderately low to moderately high range of inborn leadership capability—and that the 70 to 80 percent of us who are born in that part of the bell curve are, fortunately, quite improvable.

And the next question would be, "Well then, what does it take to improve as a leader?" In the *Leading* book, I had offered a variety of approaches for building capability in each of the six attributes outlined in the book, but as I answered this question posed by nearly all my interviewers, I noticed that I referenced four things over and over: four mental skills for learning that I had observed throughout my years of coaching and training, and that I had practiced myself. As I noticed how my responses centered on these four elements, I started to get excited: each of the four was simple, explicable, replicable. I began to think that I had happened upon a model for turbocharging one's ability to learn, an approach that could be enormously helpful to anyone who wanted to acquire new capabilities, not just in leadership, but in any area of knowledge or skill.

And given that I was, at the same time, coming to understand that the ability to acquire new skills and knowledge is the key skill of our time—for all the reasons I talked about in the first couple of chapters—I began to think that I had stumbled on something very important.

I called out these four skills of mastery and named them as I understood them:

Aspiration
Neutral self-awareness
Endless curiosity
Willingness to be bad first

I started incorporating these ANEW skills, these four elements of "mastery mindset," into my coaching practice and into my company's leadership and management training. These elements resonated with our clients, who were able to use them to improve their ability to learn new skills and knowledge quickly and well.

At that point, I decided to start working with a researcher to find out whether my hypotheses would be borne out by work being done in neuroscience, psychology, and sociology. I got even more excited: much of what Mollie West, my research assistant, and I discovered was fully aligned with what I had understood and applied empirically in our coaching and training practice. The idea of this book was born as a way to share this model and its application with a wider audience.

Back to Michelangelo—and Us

To give you an initial understanding of what these four elements entail, let's use Michelangelo's experience with the Sistine Chapel. First, I'll briefly explain the four elements of the ANEW model—*aspiration*, *neutral self-awareness*, *endless curiosity*, and *willingness to be bad first*—and then I'll describe how Michelangelo employed them to master this whole new area of endeavor . . . and what's more, to master it at a world-class level.

Aspiration

Aspiration is, put most simply, wanting something you don't now have. Great learners unearth and then build their aspiration, their own desire to learn. In order to understand why this is important, it's necessary to recognize an essential truth about human beings: we only do those things we want to do. This is a difficult idea to accept, because we've all said (and believed) at one point or another that we definitely want to do things but just haven't gotten around to them yet. But let's be accurate here: if you say you want to do something, and yet you don't do it, then that means you don't really want to do it. At least not enough to make the effort required.

This is not simply a semantic discussion. We get ourselves into all kinds of trouble, learning-wise, by telling ourselves that we want to learn things we don't really want to learn. For example, I've often noticed with coaching clients that they tell me they really want to get better at something—delegating, for instance, or financial management—but then don't make the effort to improve. And when I point out to them that it looks like they don't really want to change, since they're not changing, they often respond, "Oh, no, I really *want* to, it's just that…" It's critical to be honest with yourself about your initial level of aspiration around learning a topic, so that you'll know what you need to do in order to succeed. I'll share much more about this in the next chapter, but for the moment I'd like to ask you to go with me here: assume that whether you think you want to learn something or you think you don't—if you've been thinking about it for a while and haven't made the effort to learn it, you actually don't want to learn it that much. You lack sufficient *aspiration.*

The very good news, however, is that aspiration is not a given; you can *make yourself want to do things*, including wanting to learn new things. This is also a surprise to most people: we think that we either want to do something or we don't, and there's not much we can do about it. But, if you think about it, you've probably seen this shift—from not wanting to do something to wanting to do it—in yourself or in those around you without even realizing it. Recently, someone on our administrative team at Proteus volunteered to take on a new project. But there was one part of it—coming up with topics for a social media chat group—that she really didn't want to do; she asked if one of the consultants could do that and simply "feed" her the topics. We agreed. However, after she had talked to the person who had previously been managing the group and found out more about it, she felt very differently—she really wanted to create the topics herself. We were thrilled; she jumped right into it and has done a great job. Nothing changed about the task or the goal—only her mindset shifted; her aspiration increased.

In the next chapter, we'll dive into this: what makes us want to do or not want to do things, and how you can change your own mindset to rev up your aspiration engine when it comes to wanting to learn new things. The secret to making yourself want something lies in figuring out how acquiring the new capability will benefit you, personally, and then envisioning a future where you're reaping those benefits.

Michelangelo and Aspiration

Let's look at how Michelangelo generated the necessary aspiration to paint the Sistine Chapel ceiling. For two years, he had resisted taking on the project because he simply didn't want to do it. His aspiration was near zero. He didn't consider himself a painter, he had never worked in fresco, and he much preferred sculpture as a medium. But once it became clear that he had no choice, Michelangelo found his motivation by focusing on the ways in which it could be beneficial to him to complete the project, benefits that were meaningful to him. For example, he bargained with the pope in order to make sure he would have the chance to create his own design for the project. Michelangelo loved designing, and was excited by the idea of figuring out how to tell such a complex and meaningful story in his own way. He once said of design, "The science of design... is the source and very essence of painting, sculpture, architecture... Sometimes... it seems to me that... all the works of the human brain and hand are either design itself or a branch of that art." Given that, you can imagine how very motivating it would have been for him to know he could create his own design for the Sistine ceiling.

He also focused on the opportunity the project offered to solve a number of intriguing technical problems, something about which he had always been enthusiastic. He considered himself an engineer as much as a sculptor, and got intrigued with the idea that this project could give him the chance to come up with new ways of addressing important physical challenges.

Finally, he envisioned a future where those benefits would be his, where he would have successfully completed his own great design, having overcome the physical and technical challenges inherent in the complicated and unique space. As he wrote to a friend shortly after convincing the pope to allow him to design the project as he wished, "Now I am content that this great work will be as it should and must be." By discovering ways in which the project could give him benefits that were personally meaningful to him, and envisioning a future where he would have reaped those benefits, Michelangelo sparked his own aspiration.

Neutral Self-Awareness

When masters of mastery embark on new learning, they are accurate about where they're starting from, and they observe themselves and their strengths and weaknesses in a fair and dispassionate way. That's what we mean by neutral self-awareness. In other words, if excellent learners are bad at something, they acknowledge it—and they acknowledge any feelings they may have about that lack of skill (embarrassment, frustration, etc.) without judging, rationalizing, or avoiding them. They also know when they're good at something, and they are pretty accurate about how good or how bad they are relative to others, or relative to what's needed. In other words, great learners are what we call "fair witnesses" of themselves. (I'll explain a lot more about this in chapter 5, but it basically means they see themselves objectively and accurately.)

Cultivating neutral self-awareness is key to learning because if you don't have it, it's virtually impossible to see clearly what you need to learn or what learning those things will require from you. Let's say, for instance, that I think I'm a great people manager but I'm not. It will be difficult for me to take advantage of learning opportunities if they're presented to me (a colleague offers to give me some tips, say, or my manager lets me know the company will pay for my attendance at a management skills training program), because I won't think I need them. One of our consultants at Proteus recently worked with a coachee who, when asked what he saw as his key strengths as a leader, said that he was fair, supportive, and clear. Those who worked for him had listed the *lack* of those qualities as his key weaknesses: they reported that he played favorites, was negative, and didn't provide a good sense of what he wanted from them. That was a tough coaching engagement: the coach first had to spend a good deal of time helping the person see himself more accurately before she could begin to work with him on learning to behave differently in his areas of weakness.

In contrast, when someone is clear about where he is starting from, learning can start immediately. I just recently began coaching someone whose colleagues had offered some very tough feedback—although she was extremely smart and highly experienced, others saw her as hard to work for: critical and impatient; dismissive of others' ideas; and in the habit of taking over projects she had delegated that weren't going the way she thought they should. I was worried about how she'd receive the feedback. *If she doesn't have much in the way of neutral self-awareness*, I thought to myself, *this is going to be rough.* However, when I asked her to self-assess, her view was surprisingly aligned with the way others saw her. So when I then shared with her the feedback summary from her peers, boss, and direct reports, she simply nodded and said, "Yup. That's pretty much what I thought. It's embarrassing, but that's why I'm here: What do I do about this?" A high level of neutral self-awareness is a coach's dream—it means you can head straight into needed learning.

So what gets in the way of accurate self-perception? We'll talk about this in much greater depth in chapter 5, but the main problem is that we talk *to* ourselves *about* ourselves in ways that aren't accurate or helpful. We call that internal monologue "self-talk," and it's key to the way we see ourselves. If that voice in our head tells us, *I'm a great manager—my people may not think so, but what do they know? They're junior and have unrealistic expectations*, it's unlikely that we'll be open to new learning about how to manage. And our self-talk can be equally inaccurate and unhelpful in the opposite direction: if your mental monologue runs a continuous loop of *I'm a terrible manager, and I'll just never be good at it*, it's also unlikely that you'll be open to new learning.

The very good news is that you can manage your self-talk. You can learn to speak to yourself in ways that will allow you to see yourself clearly, and therefore position yourself to be a high-payoff learner.

In chapter 5, we'll look at a simple, realistic process for changing your self-talk in order to be more accurate about your strengths and weaknesses, especially relative to new skills or knowledge you're trying to learn. We'll also talk about "sources"—those people who see you clearly and are willing to be honest with you about what they see. Once you've got your self-talk shifted into "neutral," you can take tremendous advantage of having those people in your life… their accurate and supportive third-party feedback can be invaluable in your learning process.

Michelangelo and Neutral Self-Awareness

Once Michelangelo had found his aspiration and was motivated to move forward, he objectively assessed his strengths and weaknesses relative to the project. In other words, he took an inventory of the skills and experience he had—or didn't have—that would be essential to completing the ceiling: what he knew and knew how to do, and what he didn't. As a result, he hired assistants who had experience he lacked, primarily in the area of painting. He also wrote to a variety of colleagues to get advice about the techniques of fresco painting, especially on large surfaces, with which he had almost no experience. At the same time, he realized he could take full advantage of his knowledge as a sculptor and anatomist to make the hundreds of figures in his painting extraordinarily lifelike, and that he could combine that with his skill as an architect to envision how to make best use of the vast space, with its variety of angles and planes.

For someone so incredibly skilled in a wide variety of realms,

Michelangelo was also remarkably willing to be accurate about the areas in which he lacked skill and expertise, and very straightforward about how frustrating and demoralizing that was for him. That "fair witnessing" allowed him to begin the Sistine ceiling with realistic expectations, and with the support he needed in order to succeed.

Endless Curiosity

Curiosity is the impulse to explore and explain, to understand and master. It's built into all of us as children—and great learners either never lose that childhood drive, or they figure out how to reengage it as adults. Getting curious is essential to learning because, when combined with aspiration, it creates an unstoppable momentum of discovery. If you've ever stayed up late to finish a book, spent hours trying to figure out how to make something work, or asked someone many more questions about something than was polite simply because you really wanted to understand it—that's curiosity at work.

Curiosity is the engine of learning that takes us from being a cute little blob at birth to a pretty much fully fledged human being by the time we're ready to start school—someone who can walk, talk, eat, run, negotiate, make jokes, manipulate objects (and parents), speculate, and draw conclusions.

Unfortunately, once we get past childhood and into adolescence, that wonderful curiosity starts to get socialized out of us. We go from "Oooh, how does *that* work?" to "Oh, yeah, I know all about that." Being world weary and unimpressed becomes much cooler and more socially acceptable than being open about not knowing something and wanting to know more. And, for the most part, when we get to be adults the social norms about being incurious become even stronger. For example, I've noticed over the years that one of the biggest impediments to success for new managers is that they come into the job thinking that they're now supposed to have all the answers. They believe that revealing their lack of knowledge or being curious about what their employees may know that they don't know will be seen as weak, gauche, unsophisticated—childish.

And yet, every world-class learner throughout history—from Michelangelo to Norman Lear—is wildly curious, and relies upon curiosity as a core impulse to explore new and untested pathways.

You might be wondering how curiosity is different from aspiration. Aspiration supplies long-term motivation, while curiosity is moment to moment. Aspiration gets you started, catalyzing you to focus in a new area so you can achieve those real, meaningful benefits that you believe will come with mastering that area. Curiosity, though, is the thing that keeps you plugging away day in and day out, on a granular level. It's like a constant small itch that can only be scratched by finding out more, understanding better, becoming more skilled in an area. Aspiration makes you find a mentor; curiosity keeps you up till midnight reading the book she gave you.

And, as with aspiration, you can make yourself curious—and most people don't realize that. Just as we tend to believe that we either aspire toward something or we don't, and there's not much we can do about it, we think that we're curious about things or we aren't, period. We say, "That bores me" or "I don't care about that," as though those feelings are irrevocable. But, as with aspiration, you can learn to reengage your own curiosity, to become curious about things you need to learn, and also to reestablish a more curious habit of mind overall, which will serve you every day of your life. In chapter 6, we'll focus on how to rediscover and reengage your childhood curiosity, to reclaim that capability that's inherent in you and harness it in the service of becoming a master learner.

Michelangelo and Endless Curiosity

When Michelangelo was told that it would be difficult, if not impossible, to build traditional scaffolding, from the floor to the height required, he didn't give up—he started to wonder about what approach might work instead. He speculated that it might be possible to suspend scaffolding from the walls. And he followed his curiosity, experimenting with a variety of approaches until he invented a system that had never before been tried, and that worked so well that not a single worker was killed or seriously injured during the entire four years of work on the ceiling (a very different outcome than for other building projects in that time).

He also got curious about whether it would be possible to tell the biblical story of creation in a more compelling way, while still including its complexity and richness, rather than using the simplistic and much less ambitious design proposed by the pope. According to his biographer, Ascanio Condivi, Michelangelo pored over the Old Testament again and again, to satisfy his curiosity about all the aspects of the creation story, so that he could craft a cohesive visual framing of that story that would make best use of the entire chapel ceiling.

Finally, he used his curiosity to carry him past his frustration at his lack of expertise. At one point, he had his assistants tear out a huge section of the completed ceiling because it wasn't up to his extraordinary standards, artistically; they ended up removing almost six months' worth of work. Instead of giving up, though, or simply redoing it in the same way, he focused on figuring out how to improve that section, and came up with both a revised design and an improved plastering technique that made his second attempt significantly better.

Willingness to Be Bad First

You already know how important and difficult I think it is for us to be bad first. Most of us really dislike going back to the novice state—especially in areas where we consider ourselves experts—and we will go to great lengths to avoid being bad, looking bad, or thinking that we're bad. It's especially important to have effective tools for "being bad," because it can be very tough to overcome our resistance to being a beginner—that state of feeling embarrassed, clueless, incompetent, and just plain dumb. I spent many years working closely with someone for whom "being bad" was painfully difficult. I watched her tie herself in mental and emotional knots to avoid being perceived as anything less than expert; I watched her blame others for her mistakes or simply refuse to acknowledge them; I watched her dismiss the need to learn new skills, new approaches, or new technologies because she was caught in her own trap of not wanting to acknowledge that there was anything worthwhile that she wasn't already good at doing.

Masters of mastery figure out how to be okay with their initial ineptitude. They get, as my client said at the beginning of chapter 1, "comfortable with being uncomfortable." I'm convinced, based on my own experience, my observations of clients and colleagues, and the research we've done in this area, that the willingness to be bad first, to spend time in the "novice state," is the most potentially powerful capability you can develop as a learner.

A client and friend of mine (you'll get to know her quite well in chapter 7), an extraordinarily bright and successful woman who is remarkably sanguine about being bad first, can laugh at herself and say, "Oh my god, I'm terrible at this," without missing a beat. The secret is that she can then add, "but I know I'll get better—I'll work at it." Because that's what great learners do in this realm: they learn to accept that they'll be bad at things that are new to them, while at the very same moment believing that they'll be able to improve in those things over time.

In chapter 7, we'll dive into how to use your self-talk (the self-talk management skills you learn in chapter 5 will come in handy throughout the rest of the ANEW model) to support "being bad" in the most useful way possible, and we'll also explore a technique that great learners use—an approach we call "bridging"—that gives you a way to take best advantage of your current experience as you learn new things.

Michelangelo and Willingness to Be Bad First

Michelangelo was already renowned as an artist when he began the Sistine Chapel—he was an expert by any measure. Michelangelo may not have enjoyed having to go outside his expertise (his lack of experience as a painter, and specifically as a frescoist, was the main reason he tried to decline the project), but he put that aside to plunge into the reality of initially "being bad." One of his biographers noted that, at the beginning of the project, he was often heard to call down to his assistants, saying, "I am no artist—come up and help me." He fully accepted his lack of skill at the beginning of the project. As I noted earlier, he had his assistants strip out great sections of early work that weren't as he'd envisioned them, saying, "If the wine is bad, throw it out!" At the same time, he had faith in his own ability to learn, to overcome the challenges of the project in order to create something wonderful, saying, "Faith in oneself is the best and safest course."

Starting from this balanced mindset of "I'm bad now, but I can get good," he then leveraged what he already knew and had learned, using it as a "bridge" on which to build his new, related, learning. For example, he was able to think, *I understand how bodies are constructed, from my work in anatomy and sculpture, so I can apply that to learning how to represent figures realistically in two-dimensional space.*

Michelangelo's ability to accept his lack of experience and skill in some areas, and to know that mistakes and misunderstanding were inevitable; his self-belief; and his ability to bridge from his existing knowledge in learning new skills: these three elements combined to support him in learning astonishingly quickly, so that by the end of the four-year Sistine Chapel project he was considered among the best fresco painters alive.

Completely Within Your Control

Before we dive into the rest of the book, where you'll learn how to increase your ability in each of these four mindset skills, I'd like to point something else out to you. In my review of Michelangelo's use of the ANEW skills, I've not spoken much about his unique talent or his previous experience as a working artist. While his talent and experience were, of course, essential to his success in painting the Sistine Chapel, they would not have been sufficient if he hadn't also had the mindset of a learner. No matter what preexisting knowledge, experience, or talent you bring to learning something new, you still need these "ANEW" capabilities.

And, to our great good fortune, these skills of mental awareness and discipline are available to everyone, no matter her preexisting talent, training, circumstance, or environment. I'm convinced that anyone who wants to can become a skilled learner of new capabilities. In other words, the ANEW skills are yours if you want them.

I'm assuming that you do. I'm assuming that if you've read this far, you want to jump into the twenty-first century, take a header into the huge river of knowledge and possibility that exists around us and within us, and become the best learner you're capable of being. I assume that you want to be able to learn and change and grow for as long as you live, and that you want to become a true master of mastery so that you can take full advantage of the world and all it has to offer you, both personally and professionally.

First, Some Self-Assessment

Before we dive in and explore ANEW in more depth, I want to encourage you to spend a few minutes reflecting on your current capability in each of these four learning skills. Think of this as an initial exercise in increasing your neutral self-awareness. You can go to bebadfirst.com and download a writeable PDF worksheet to use in completing this and the other exercises throughout the book. (Or, if you like the old-school approach, create a "be bad first" notebook to use for writing your responses to the activities throughout the book and any other notes you might want to take along the way.)

TRY IT

My current state as a master of mastery:

Score yourself 1–5 in each of the four areas, with **1** being "I do this rarely or not well" and **5** being "I do this consistently and very well."

Aspiration: How good am I at getting myself to want to do things?

①   ②   ③   ④   ⑤

Neutral self-awareness: How accurate am I in assessing my strengths and weaknesses and how I feel about them?

①   ②   ③   ④   ⑤

Endless curiosity: How much do I access my own inborn curiosity?

①   ②   ③   ④   ⑤

Willingness to be bad first: How willing am I to be in the beginner state?

①   ②   ③   ④   ⑤

It's good to have this initial hypothesis about where you're starting from as a learner to use as a benchmark. (You can also take a more in-depth assessment, at bebadfirst.com, that will offer some insight into your current level of skill in the ANEW skills and some insights about how to improve.)

And Some Real Topics

Finally, before we leave this chapter, I'd like you to roll up your mental sleeves and prepare to apply the concepts we're discussing by drawing from your own life. My hope for you, as I've said from the beginning, is that by the end of our time together, you'll be a significantly better learner: that you'll have substantively improved your ability to learn new things quickly and well. We've found over the years, in coaching executives and training managers and leaders, that trying out new skills in a real-to-you situation is the best context for acquiring them.

In the service of creating a solid basis for your development of the ANEW skills, I'd like you to think about and note two learning opportunities that are real for you now.

TRY IT

What's one thing that you're excited about learning—something you want to learn?
(Ideally, this would be something you've already started learning, since that's your best indication that you really do want to learn it!)

What's one thing that you know you need to learn, but that you don't want to learn?
(This can be something that you already know you don't want to learn. It can also be something that you think or say you want to learn...but that you haven't yet been able to make consistent effort to learn.)

We'll use these two learning opportunities as real-to-you situations for practicing the ANEW skills throughout the rest of the book. I'll also be offering you lots of examples, as I have in this chapter.

A few more questions, before we move on: Are you starting to want to explore these ideas? Are you a little clearer about where your growth areas might be? Are you wondering what's next? Are you acknowledging that you might not be as good at learning new things as you'd like to be?

If so, you're already on the ANEW path. Let's keep going.

CHAPTER 4

Aspiration: Ya Gotta Wanna

...The artist had been resisting the pope's commission for a number of reasons. First, he considered himself primarily a sculptor rather than a painter, and didn't want to spend years on a gigantic project that he didn't feel he was best suited to complete. He also didn't like the pope's design for the ceiling (and that's a hard thing to say to a pope). Finally, he knew that, should he take the job, it would involve years of uncomfortable, painstaking labor.

But once he realized there was no avoiding the pope's "request," Michelangelo began to figure out how to make the best of it. First he negotiated for and finally received permission to create a much more intricate and grand design than the one envisioned by the pope. Next, he became engrossed in solving the purely technical problems presented by the task: how to adapt the techniques of fresco (painting with a colored wash on damp plaster) to a gigantic space (133 by 46 feet), while suspended almost 70 feet from the ground.

By the time Michelangelo had permission to, in his words, "do as he liked" in terms of the design, and had created what he believed were viable solutions for the technical problems presented by the project, his attitude had changed dramatically—he told friends he could hardly wait to get started...

Wanting and Not Wanting

You may have read that snippet above, from my account of Michelangelo and the Sistine Chapel, and thought, *Well, sure, I could learn all kinds of things, if I really wanted to—but I don't want to.*

And part of that is true. As I noted earlier, we human beings only do what we want to do. However, we make some assumptions related to this fact that get in our way and make it more difficult for us to learn and grow.

First, we assume that if we don't want to do something, it's permanent—that we can't change our level of "wanting." We'll spend most of this chapter talking about why that's not true, and what you can do to change your level of aspiration, as Michelangelo did. But before we dig into that topic, I want to point out and set aside two other ways we muddy the aspiration waters with false assumptions.

Saying We Want What We Don't (**Really**)

The first false assumption we often make about aspiration, which I mentioned briefly in the last chapter, is believing we want to do things that we don't actually want to do. A friend and colleague of mine, Jim, has been telling himself (and others) for years that he really wants to learn to play the piano. But he hasn't done it. I asked him why he hasn't pursued it, given that he says he really wants to learn, and his very honest answer was, "I don't know." He went on to say, "I've bought books and music, I have a keyboard…I can't figure out why I haven't done anything about it." I pointed out to him that if there's nothing getting in the way of his learning to play, and yet he's not doing it, then he doesn't really want to do it. We often confuse *being interested in the possibility* of something with actually *wanting to achieve it.*

Apply this to yourself. Think about something that you've said to yourself or other people that you want to do, but that you haven't actually made any effort to pursue. If you're honest with yourself, I believe you'll recognize that you probably have a kind of vague idea that this would be a cool or fun or useful thing to do or know, rather than having a clear drive to accomplish mastery in that area. That's the difference between interest and aspiration. Here's one example that applies to most people. I once read about a survey taken of adults of varying ages and demographics in the United States, in which they were asked if they someday wanted to write a book. More than four out of five of them (84 percent) said, "Yes, definitely." Given that only some very small percentage of adults actually do write books, this "wanting" is clearly, for the most part, a mild interest in the possibility of writing a book rather than a true aspiration to do so, one that will carry the person forward into the actual effort required to become an author.

This distinction is far more than idle wordsmithery. Being accurate about whether or not you actually aspire to learn something is essential. If you keep telling yourself that you want to learn something that you actually don't want to learn, your efforts to learn will assume your "wanting" is already in place—like my friend Jim, you'll buy books, sign up for classes, make to-do lists, and set goals. But you're likely to find those efforts ineffective, because they won't address your underlying "not wanting to" problem. They won't help you increase your fundamental level of aspiration.

Saying We Don't Want to When We Do (Kind Of)

The second way we confuse ourselves about the true nature of aspiration is that we sometimes do things while believing and saying that we *don't* want to do them. I can almost hear you thinking, for instance, *Hold on now, how can you say we only do the things we want to do? I clean the downstairs bathroom every week, and I absolutely don't want to do that.* But I submit to you that you must want it more than you want the alternatives (a progressively more disgusting bathroom, or possibly a progressively more irritated spouse or room-mate), or you wouldn't do it. When we do something we don't want to do very much, it's because we see it (usually without consciously thinking this through) as the best option available; we believe we'll gain something important (or avoid something bad) by doing it. In other words, you can bitch all you want to about how much you hate to exercise or clean the bathroom, but if you're actually exercising or cleaning the bathroom, it means you want to get the benefits from doing it (or avoid the bad outcomes of not doing it) more than you hate doing it.

Think about anything that you don't like but do anyway. I'll bet you a hundred dollars that you want the outcome from doing that thing more than you want the outcome from not doing it.

So: We Do What We Want Most

To summarize, with a nuance that takes into account both of these situations: *we only do those things that we want to do more than any other option that's available to us in a given situation.*

Unfortunately for us, in most situations where we would really benefit from learning something new, there's almost always another option available to us that seems less onerous and difficult. That option: staying with the tried and true. That's what Michelangelo wanted to do. He wanted to keep being a sculptor and not have to learn to paint a giant fresco, suspended upside down seventy feet off the ground. In fact, the project he kept trying to convince Pope Julius to sign off on, instead of the Sistine ceiling, was the design and creation of a huge and complex marble tomb for the pope, something Michelangelo envisioned as a tour de force of his sculptor's art.

And here in the twenty-first century, with everyone's job changing on a daily basis, this wanting-to-stay-with-the-tried-and-true resistance to learning or doing new things happens continuously. For example, let's say there's a librarian named Ron, and his library is in the process of digitizing every piece of paper in its collection and then making those digitized files easily accessible to all its patrons. He thinks he could probably learn all the skills required to do that. However, it would take a good deal of time and energy, and also Ron isn't a big fan of learning new software programs. Basically, he'd simply rather not do it. So, instead, he decides to keep doing the thing he wants to do more: focusing on the traditional part of his job, at which he feels very competent. He likes (and is good at) caring for the books and other materials in the library's collection and helping library patrons find and use them. He wants to keep doing his job the way he's always done it.

Now, an important point here: I bet Ron is not consciously aware of his resistance to this new possibility; he's probably not saying (aloud or to himself) that he doesn't want to learn the new skills he needs in order to be involved in the digitization effort. In fact, he may even tell himself—and others—that he *does* want to do it. But then, somehow, he just never has time, or he convinces himself that his boss needs him to focus on the more traditional parts of the job. (This is one of the more dangerous aspects of being confused about our "wanting and not wanting"—we rarely admit to ourselves that we don't want to do something that we think we *should* do. We simply tell ourselves that other people's agendas, a lack of time or money, or our "poor discipline" are making it impossible for us to do the thing.)

Unfortunately for Ron, though, some of his colleagues will either want to learn the new approach or will overcome their resistance to wanting to learn it. And eventually, (sorry, but it's true) he'll be out of a job. Long before that, though, he'll be relegated to a kind of employment backwater, where his skills will become gradually less useful and less transferable to other jobs. Ron will also most likely be taking himself out of the running for advancement in his career: he will have effectively marginalized himself professionally.

Remember when I said, in earlier chapters, that the ability to learn well and continuously is the key skill of the twenty-first century? This is a great example of what I was talking about. If you go with the path of least resistance when it comes to learning—that is, if you avoid learning new and uncomfortable things—the world will pass you by.

How to Make Yourself Want Something

Remember, though, that you *can* make yourself want to do things—including wanting to learn things you don't now want to learn. You can, in effect, ignite your own aspiration. Here's how it works.

To make yourself want to learn something:

➤ Imagine the personal benefits to you of learning it
➤ Envision a "possible world" where you're enjoying those benefits

These two things are core to human motivation. When we do anything that requires effort—from walking to the corner store to buy milk to getting an MBA—we do it because we see clearly how it will benefit us, and we imagine the future where we're reaping those benefits. (*I only like to eat cereal with milk, and that new cereal will be delicious with milk on it*, or *I want to move up in the organization, and I think an MBA will help. With an MBA, I can see myself as a senior executive.*)

When we don't want to do something, we tend to think and talk about the difficulties and obstacles of doing it. Shifting your focus toward the potential benefits of learning a new thing—and the positive future that could result—is a simple and powerful way of igniting your aspiration.

How Aspiration Looks

To give you a real-life sense of the importance of engaging your "aspiration muscles" in today's work world, let me introduce you to a client of ours, Detavio Samuels. I first met Detavio when he had just been offered a big new job, one that hadn't previously existed. Alfred Liggins, CEO of Radio One, a leading U.S.-based urban media company, had invited Detavio to become president of One Solution, a new division tasked with integrating the advertising sales of all the Radio One assets: dozens of radio stations in major markets across the country; the TV One television network; Interactive One, a portfolio of urban-focused online properties; and Reach Media, a creator and distributor of syndicated content for radio.

Detavio had previously been president of the Detroit office of GlobalHue, a multicultural advertising agency, so I realized this new job was going to present a steep learning curve for him. Though he knew the advertising industry extremely well, the businesses of Radio One—especially the radio stations—were going to be new to him in lots of ways. When offered the position, he could easily have focused on all the ways in which it would be different from (and therefore more risky and difficult than) his current job, and decided not to make the effort required. So in that first conversation, I asked him why he had wanted this new job.

"I know it's going to take a lot—but it will give me a chance to build on what I know," he said. "I've only seen these media businesses from the agency side—looking at them as places for our clients to advertise—and now I'll get to understand them from the inside out. That's exciting to me. And I love having the opportunity to build something new—we can create something that hasn't been done before at Radio One . . . or maybe anywhere. And I get the feeling that Alfred will give me a lot of leeway and support—he's hiring me to take this in a new direction. And if we can make this all work, it will benefit everyone: the whole company, our consumers and advertisers—and me!"

At that moment, I thought to myself, *This guy is great at aspiration.* In those few sentences, Detavio demonstrated that he was focusing on the personal benefits to him of the new learning that would be required of him: that he'd have the chance to build on his existing learning; create something new; and have a lot of responsibility in that endeavor—and on the future in which he and others would be enjoying those benefits.

He took the job, and I watched as he dove into that new learning, his strong aspiration overcoming the attendant obstacles and frustrations. He's well on his way to making One Solution a growth catalyst for the entire company.

Imagining the Benefits

Let's deconstruct what Detavio did, to help you get more adept at aspiration. When faced with an opportunity to either learn something new or stay in his comfort zone, Detavio first focused on how learning the new thing would benefit him. He noted that being able to build on his existing business knowledge, having the chance to create something new, and being offered freedom and support were all very attractive to him.

One thing I noticed in my conversations with Detavio: he was very clear about what was motivating to him, not only in this situation but in his life in general. I've noticed that this is true of good learners—they tend to be consciously aware of what they like and don't like to do, which makes it easier for them to ramp up their aspiration when necessary. They can look for the potential benefits in the "don't want to yet" situation that they know will be motivating to them.

One simple way to find out what motivates you, if you haven't thought about this much before, is to look at something you do want to learn—as evidenced by the fact that you're making effort to learn it—and think about what benefits you're getting (or will get) from learning that thing. You might want to look at a few different things you've learned or are learning, so you can start to see the pattern of what motivates you.

Then, once you have a clearer understanding of the benefits that are most important to you in doing new things, you can look to see if these benefits might be available in a situation where you don't yet want to learn—where your aspiration isn't yet sufficient.

Here's what my friend Jim found when he did this exercise. Though he hadn't been able to "want" to learn the piano enough to actually do it, he *had* begun to learn to play golf. When I asked him what benefits he was deriving from that, he responded, "I like feeling physically challenged—like I'm teaching my body to do new things. I also like being out in the fresh air. And I really like doing it with my son—the social aspect of it is important to me." After we talked a bit more, he realized that, while the second benefit (getting outside) wasn't easily available in learning to play the piano, both teaching his body to do new things and learning with someone else were available to him in learning the piano. He began to figure out how he could incorporate those benefits into his learning approach.

And here's a workplace example: one of our consultants at Proteus, Cindy, was hesitant about learning to facilitate our vision and strategy process. She had talked for a few years about possibly wanting to learn, but didn't take any steps in that direction; she clearly didn't want to do it enough to commit to making the necessary effort. Then, at one point, she told us she'd like to start the certification process. I asked her what had changed. "I realized I was focusing on what would be hard about it, and on the possibility that

I wouldn't be as good at it as I'd want to be," she said. "But then I thought about what a great way it is to help clients be successful, which is so important to me. And I also thought about how much I've enjoyed, over the past few years, gaining skills and insights that I didn't have before. I realized that learning this process would offer me both of those things in spades." Cindy recently completed her certification process and conducted her first solo vision and strategy session, to rave reviews from the client.

TRY IT

Now you'll have a chance to flex your own "aspiration muscles." Look back at the topic you noted in the last chapter that you do want to learn—one that, ideally, you have already started learning. Focus on what benefits you hope to achieve (or have already begun to achieve) from learning it. This will probably be relatively easy for you to do; since you actually do want to learn this thing, you've already recognized the benefits to you on some level, although you may not have thought about it consciously. You can note your answers in the PDF you downloaded from bebadfirst.com or in your notebook.

Benefits I hope to gain (or am I gaining) from learning in this area where I do want to learn:

Getting clearer about those benefits that are most important to you is valuable in two ways. It gives you a better sense of how you're wired aspirationally—what's likely to be motivating to you in any situation. You can also use this understanding of yourself—as Detavio, Jim, and Cindy did—to increase your aspiration in your "don't want to" areas. Thinking through how you might gain some of these same benefits in those areas helps you break the unhelpful cycle of thinking only about the difficulties and obstacles (which is what we tend to focus on when thinking about things we don't want to learn).

TRY IT

With your example in mind, think about the thing you don't yet want to learn. How could learning that thing offer you some of the same benefits? Note your responses on your PDF or in your notebook. (This is the last time I'll say that—I'm sure you've got the drill by now!)

How could the thing I don't want to learn offer me some of the benefits I identified in the previous exercise (or other benefits that are equally important to me)?

Imagining a Possible World

When I was first talking with Detavio, he focused on the future world where he'd be enjoying the benefits he envisioned. He was—and continues to be—very excited about a future where he's deeply knowledgeable about the Radio One businesses and where that knowledge is allowing him to work with others to drive the company's revenues and broaden its scope.

That's the second part of this skill of aspiration—learning to envision possible futures where you've gained the benefits you recognize. The core of this capability relies upon the fact that all humans are able to envision a future that doesn't now exist. Any kid who's ever wanted a bike for her birthday has done it: that kid knows just what the bike will look like, how it will feel to ride it down the street, and how her friends will react the first time they see it.

Unfortunately, we're all equally capable of quashing that capability by focusing on the difficulties in achieving our vision. (*I'll never get that bike*, or *I'm such a klutz I'll probably fall off in front of all my friends.*) The art of envisioning a possible positive future lies in being able to access your own visioning capability without getting in the way of it. That getting-in-the-way is what happens, generally, when we don't want to learn something, especially if it's something we know we *need* to learn but are resisting. Rather than envisioning a future where we're reaping the benefits of having learned it, we focus on all the difficulties and obstacles that could get in the way of attaining that future success, and our aspiration takes a nosedive.

I talk about the power of envisioning a hoped-for future in much more detail in some of my other books, most specifically in *Being Strategic*. I invite you to read that more in-depth exploration of this area if you know this is a place where you especially need to develop. For now, though, here's a condensed version of that model, focused on learning. In order to support yourself to completely envision a future where you've gained the benefits of new learning:

1. Pick a time frame for success.
2. Imagine yourself in that future.
3. Describe what success looks and feels like.
4. Select the key elements.

1. **Pick a time frame for success.** Begin by deciding on a reasonable time frame for success, a point by which you could reasonably expect to be reaping the benefits of your new learning. It's important that you pick a time frame that's realistic—otherwise, you won't believe it's possible and your envisioned future will have much less power to motivate you to take the actions needed to get there. For example, you might choose a one-month time frame for learning that new spreadsheet program, while a six- or twelve-month time frame might be more appropriate for substantially improving your leadership skills.

2. **Imagine yourself in that future.** This is where you access your own power to envision the future, and focus it on the benefits you've identified. To do so, you need to give your mind free rein to create a three-dimensional piece of a possible future where you're experiencing those benefits. To do that, put yourself into a mental time machine. Imagine emerging from your time machine into the same room and the same chair you're sitting in now, but on the date you've chosen above in step 1. You've returned to this room, this chair, to celebrate the fact that you've created your hoped-for future: you've learned the new skill or capability, and are reaping the benefits you hoped to gain. You can support your envisioning with a simple statement that lets your brain access its visionary mode. For example: "It's now March of 20xx, and I'm reflecting on my success in having learned _____." Once you feel comfortably settled into this possible world, go on to the next step.

3. **Describe what success looks and feels like.** As you mentally look around this new world at the end of your time travels, what do you see? Think about the benefits you identified, and imagine that they've come to pass: describe what that looks, feels, and sounds like. (For instance, if you're envisioning a future where you've learned presentation skills, it might be something like: *I'm making a business presentation to my boss and his peers, and I'm clear, focused, and relaxed. My body language and voice are strong and assured, and I handle their unexpected questions well. I feel proud of myself, and my boss congratulates me on a job well done.*) Some people like to visualize these things, others like to talk them through aloud, but it's generally helpful, in either case, to jot down your thoughts.

4. **Select the key elements.** When you feel you have a fairly robust picture of this future you want, review what you've written and select the key elements, those parts of the future that are the most enticing and motivating to you. I suggest you choose a few

items that best indicate to you that you've gained the benefits you hoped for. (For example, in the example above, you might pick out "I'm a skilled and relaxed presenter," "I know how to respond to the unexpected," and "Both my boss and I are pleased and proud.")

TRY IT

Now I encourage you to try this in the area where you don't want to learn, drawing on the potential benefits you described above to envision a realistic possible world.

Envisioning a "hoped-for future" where I'm reaping the benefits of my learning...

    Pick a time frame (when I will be much more skilled or knowledgeable in this area):

Imagine yourself in that future, and describe what success looks and feels like (how I feel and what I'm doing, having gained the benefits from this learning):

Select the key elements (how I'm experiencing my hoped-for benefits in this future world of successful learning):

Now that you've had a chance to catalyze your own aspiration in this area, take a minute to stop and reflect: How are you now feeling about learning this new skill or capability?

I hope you're feeling a bit more interested than at the beginning of the chapter—perhaps you're thinking about ways to make time to learn or people you can talk to who could help. Maybe you're even feeling a little excited.

That's the power of aspiration. Wanting something is a tremendously potent force. It turns our attention almost automatically from looking at all the reasons we can't do something—all the ways it will be scary or boring, time consuming or complicated—to focusing on how we can make it happen in spite of any difficulties. Once we've seen how something can give us benefits that are important to us, and then envisioned a future in which we're enjoying those benefits, we start looking for ways we can create opportunities to make that future a reality. I've found it's almost magical, that shift in focus that unleashes a person's aspiration.

One of the most exciting examples of that "aspiration magic" I've ever experienced happened about ten years ago. I was coaching the CEO of a company that was growing rapidly from small to midsized. He was a great operator, very smart and experienced, and the business was focused and well organized as a result. The problem was that he had gotten to a point where he really needed to start letting go of the day-to-day operations. He needed—badly—to delegate more of his key responsibilities to the folks who worked for him, because as the business got larger and more complex, he was becoming a bottleneck. All the important decisions were still going through him, and even though he had lots of energy and intelligence, it just wasn't possible for him to keep up. It was frustrating and demoralizing for his executives as well, and I knew he was about to lose one of his key folks if he didn't change. We had talked about the issue at length, and he understood the problem intellectually. I taught him our delegation model; he didn't really use it. I started to understand that this was an aspiration problem.

So I asked him what benefits he might get from delegating more. He said, "Oh I know it's probably a good idea, but I just have high standards, and I need to make sure the most important things happen the way they need to . . . sometimes people just don't ask the right questions if I'm not around." Instead of focusing on the benefits, he was telling me all the difficulties he saw in doing it—no wonder his aspiration was nonexistent! I said, "Yeah, I know it would be tough to manage the company in a whole different way, and it seems fraught with difficulties. Humor me, though: How might it benefit you?"

He actually stopped and thought about it. "You know," he said, "if I could figure out how to get some of this stuff off my plate—and still get great results, you understand—I'd have more time to think about what we're going to need to do over the next year or two to incorporate some of this new technology into our operations. It's irritating not to have time to focus on that—and it's bad for the business." He paused for another minute, tapping his pen on the desk. "And I know Jack's frustrated. I don't want to lose him—he's my best guy. I'm sure if I stepped back from his area, he'd be a lot happier." I agreed on both counts, and we started talking about how to make it happen.

I won't say that he changed overnight, or that he changed 100 percent—to this day, he has some unhelpful tendencies toward micromanaging. But within a couple of months, most of his direct reports mentioned to me that his approach had changed significantly: he was less likely to second-guess their decisions and he had started saying, "Come to me if you have a problem with that, but otherwise it's yours to do," and sticking to it. Staff meetings had shifted from him mostly giving direction to him mostly listening to the function heads' reports and asking good and useful questions.

And that's a wonderful setup for the remaining three skills of ANEW; as soon as you start *aspiring* to learn something, you're in a much better mental space to become *neutrally self-aware, endlessly curious*, and *willing to be bad first* in that area, so that you actually can learn new skills and new ways of behaving, like my client did.

It was true for Michelangelo, it's true for Detavio Samuels and my now-better-at-delegating client, and it's true for you—aspiration is a necessary and powerful beginning—but it's just the beginning...

CHAPTER 5

Neutral Self-Awareness:
The *American Idol* Syndrome

≡ ...Because he had never worked in fresco as a mature
≡ artist, but only as an apprentice in the studio of his master
≡ Ghirlandaio, Michelangelo hired assistants, many from
≡ his old master's studio, who had more experience with the
≡ medium. They helped him figure out how to apply the tech-
≡ nique to the massive dimensions of the ceiling, and how to
≡ work on a painting surface that was arched above them...

The Challenge of Seeing Ourselves Clearly

Michelangelo seems to have had remarkably little resistance to
acknowledging his weaknesses, including his lack of current capability as a painter, and particularly as a frescoist. As I noted earlier,
he was even heard to tell assistants when he had little knowledge
or experience in a given area, and to ask for their help. Unfortunately, most of us aren't as unflinching about our strengths and
weaknesses—and that self-deception makes it much harder for us
to learn.

In fact, David Dunning, a psychologist at Cornell who writes
about the challenge of self-deception, has gathered a lot of compelling

data about how "off" we tend to be, when assessing our own current capabilities. Here are some of the high points:

High school seniors: 70 percent report having "above average" leadership skills, compared with 2 percent who report their skills as "below average." When rating their abilities to get along with others, 25 percent believe they are in the top 1 percent and 60 percent put themselves in the top 10 percent.

College professors: 94 percent think they do above-average work.

Engineers: in two different companies, more than 30 percent believe their performance is in the top 5 percent in their companies.

Doctors, and nurses: for treating thyroid disorders, handling basic life-support tasks, and performing surgery, this study of Dunning's found, there is no correlation between what health-care professionals say they know and what they actually know.[1]

It sounds like the real-life version of Garrison Keillor's Lake Wobegon, where "all the women are strong, all the men are good-looking, and all the children are above average." So—why are we so often wrong when it comes to assessing ourselves, and why is that a problem when it comes to learning?

We Say We Are Who We'd Like to Be

The main reason we don't want to acknowledge our deficits, it turns out, is that we secretly think we can't to do anything about them. Carol Dweck, a leading researcher in the field of motivation and author of *Mindset*, has talked and written extensively about what she calls "fixed mindset vs. growth mindset."[2] In her research, she's found that many people believe they are who they are: that their current capabilities and strengths are pretty fixed. With this underlying belief, it makes sense that we wouldn't want to acknowledge our lacks or deficits: if we believe that who we are right now is who we're destined to be, then, of course, we would also want to believe that who we are right now is wonderful. In other words, our unrealistically positive self-perceptions cover over our belief that we're not great now...and we're never going to be great.

My favorite example (though also very poignant) of this lack of neutral self-awareness, and the insecurities that reinforce it, is what I've come to call "the *American Idol* Syndrome." We've all seen it: those contestants on the program who cannot sing by any objective measure, and yet who tell everyone (loudly and with conviction) that they expect to win the contest and go on to become the next great American pop sensation. Because they want so much to win, and they (I suspect) believe that they're as good as they're going to get, they've convinced themselves that they are—right now—completely awesome. And so these contestants will tell the show's hosts and the American viewing public at every opportunity that they're exceptionally talented and accomplished vocalists.

I've also noticed that these folks are always astonished and resistant when the judges say, accurately, "You have a terrible singing voice—I hope you haven't quit your day job, and you are definitely not going on to the next round." In fact, when interviewed after their unsuccessful auditions, these contestants generally cling to their belief in their own capability, ascribing their failure to the judges' bias, to their own nerves, or to no one appreciating their "unique talent." In other words, they immediately re-erect their psychological defenses against acknowledging the possibility that they may simply not be good singers.

Why It Matters

It's unlikely that self-deceiving *American Idol* contestants go home the next day and call a singing teacher, saying, "I'd really love to be a great singer, but I've realized I'm not very good right now, and that I need a lot of help if I want to improve." And that's why neutral self-awareness is so important. If you want to be good at something, and yet you're not willing or able to be accurate about your current level of capability, you won't be open to doing what you need to do in order to improve.

We often run into this phenomenon as executive coaches. When someone we're coaching has an area of weakness but believes it's a strength, any suggestion we might offer to support improvement is liable to simply bounce off the person. Let's say, for instance, that a coachee thinks he's great at building strong teams, but the input you've gotten as his coach is that he's actually very bad at this. You can give him the feedback, you can explain to him the characteristics of high-performing teams, and you can offer him skills for building those characteristics on his own team...but if he's convinced he's already good at it, he's unlikely to absorb much of what you've shared. This is why, as coaches, we always put a good deal of effort at the beginning of the engagement into raising the level of neutral self-awareness of the coachee: otherwise, anything that follows is likely to be a waste of everyone's time.

Getting Clearer About Yourself

Fortunately, there's a surprisingly simple way to become aware of how you see yourself, and to shift your self-perception if it's not accurate. In other words, you can become more neutrally self-aware.

To increase your neutral self-awareness:

➤ Manage your self-talk
➤ Become your own fair witness
➤ Invite good "sources"

Neutral self-awareness starts when you gain more awareness and control over how you talk to yourself about yourself. Most people don't know that you can do this, but it's true: you can actually change your internal monologue. Once you've begun to learn the skill of managing that inner voice, you can build on that skill to become a more objective and accurate observer of your own life and capabilities—a "fair witness," if you will. And when your assessment of your current capabilities is more accurate and less defended, you can then be open to feedback coming from those around you. Then you can take the final step in building neutral self-awareness: finding people who are good sources of information about you and inviting them to share their insights with you.

How Neutral Self-Awareness Looks

The first time I spoke with Adam Stotsky, I was impressed by his level of neutral self-awareness. He had just been hired as the president of a cable TV network at NBCU that was about to undergo a major rebranding and repositioning. Adam's new boss, Bonnie Hammer, chairman of NBCUniversal Cable Entertainment Group, who had worked with Adam earlier in his career and knew him well, had asked me to engage with Adam as his coach. Although Adam had led increasingly larger and more complex marketing functions during his career, he had never run a whole business, and although Bonnie had a lot of faith in his ability to do so, she wanted to give him all the support she could, to help assure his success.

I had never met Adam, although I knew many people who knew him well, and so had a pretty good sense of how he was seen by others. If their perceptions were accurate, Adam was extremely smart, quick, and creative. His biggest weakness, according to those who knew and had worked with him, was a tendency toward what they described as "arrogance." When I asked for specifics, they noted that he had a tendency not to listen to others at times, and to assume he was right, even in situations where others had more experience or knowledge.

During our initial conversation, I wanted to make sure that he was interested in working with a coach. His response was refreshingly honest. "I'm glad Bonnie suggested it," he said. "Running a network—even a small one—will be different in lots of ways than running a marketing department. I know you've worked with CEOs and GMs, and I hope you'll be able to help me avoid some of the major pitfalls."

Since I've become so sensitive to self-awareness, or the lack thereof, in those I coach, I was pleased to hear that he recognized that his new job might require capabilities he hadn't yet developed. So I decided to push into potentially more difficult territory for him, to test the extent of his neutral self-awareness and see what might be required in our work together.

"I think you're right," I said. "This is going to be different in a bunch of ways. So what strengths do you have now, as a manager, leader, and businessperson, that you think will support your success in this job? And what weaknesses or deficits do you have that you think might get in your way?"

There was a long pause on the other end of the line. "I think I'm a reasonably good manager," he said slowly. "I give clear direction, and if people do a good job, I let them operate pretty independently—I don't think I'm a micromanager. I have good creative sensibilities, and I think I can recognize that in others. And I think I'm good at executing on a brand—three-dimensionalizing the essence of a brand." He thought for a minute. "I'm going to have to learn a lot more about programming. I'll need a great head of programming. And I've managed a marketing P&L, but I'll need to do a deeper dive to get a more complete view of how the financials work for a whole network."

I decided to push it even further. "What else?" I asked. "What would you say is your Achilles heel as a leader?" Another, even longer pause. "I know people think I'm arrogant," he said. "And I can see why they think that. I know I can come on too strong, respond too quickly, and not give people a chance to say what they think. I tend to be the first one to talk in most situations. I don't listen very well when I think I'm right about something. I'm not proud of it, but there it is."

I was thrilled. Adam seemed to have a very clear view of his key growth area, and to be willing to acknowledge it without much prompting, and without evasion or self-justification. And, even rarer, he was able to be honest with himself about how he felt about it. From my point of view as a coach and teacher, this was the optimal beginning.

Over the past few years, as Adam and I have worked together, I've seen the value of his ability to be a "fair witness" of himself over and over. His accurate assessment of his tendency toward arrogance has allowed him to be open to feedback from me and others, and he's worked hard to balance his self-confidence with more listening and greater consideration of others' input. The folks who work for him have told me—and him—that they see him as both decisive and collaborative, a wonderful combination of his existing strengths and new capability in his area of growth.

I've also seen Adam apply his neutral self-awareness in a variety of other settings. When he's tried things with the network that haven't turned out well—programs that haven't caught on with the viewers or people who haven't been a good fit for the team—he's quickly recognized and acknowledged his mistakes, and then moved to correct them. And when he or someone on his team does something well, he acknowledges that, too. It's important to be accurate in assessing your strengths and successes, as well as your weaknesses and growth areas: true neutral self-awareness allows you to leverage your existing strengths as you work to improve in your areas of growth.

Seeing himself with clear eyes has allowed Adam to learn quickly and thrive in his job—in fact, after about eighteen months, he was invited to add the job of GM for the E! network to his portfolio as a result of his success at building the Esquire Network and team. And I've seen him digging into this new part of his job in the same way: recognizing the value of the knowledge and experience he's gained running Esquire, and looking to see what he doesn't yet know that he'll need to learn in order to be successful at E!.

Managing Your Self-Talk

You may be wondering whether you're accurate in your self-perception—and what to do about it if you're not. Fortunately, it's relatively straightforward both to find out whether you're seeing yourself clearly and to increase the accuracy of your self-perception. It's not always easy (as we explore this, you may encounter some internal resistance to seeing and acknowledging the less flattering aspects of yourself), but it *is* simple—that is, not complicated. And if you make consistent use of the tools I'm about to share with you, you'll find yourself getting more and more comfortable with seeing yourself as you are.

People who see themselves clearly start by learning to manage how they talk to themselves about themselves. This may be a new idea for you—the idea of having control over how you talk to yourself—especially if you've never focused much on your own interior monologue. So, here's a fact: you have a fairly continuous mental monologue running at the back of your mind, underneath your everyday conversation and actions. Here's another—very important—fact: you can change the content of that mental monologue.

Because we're going to be focusing a great deal on this idea of self-talk throughout the rest of the book, I'd like you to take a moment and simply listen to the chatter that's going on inside your head right now. Stop reading, if you would; close your eyes, and notice what you're saying to yourself. It might take a minute to tune into it, but just sit quietly until you can "hear" it.

Okay, we're back. You may have noticed that some of what you were saying to yourself in this "inner voice" was fairly benign. (*This book is pretty interesting so far. I wonder if it will rain tomorrow. My neck hurts.*) But often, what we say to ourselves isn't benign at all. And you may have "heard" some of that kind of self-talk as you were listening just now, too. Too often, our mental monologue consists of unhelpful and inaccurate statements about ourselves and others. (*That guy's an idiot. I'll never be able to be a great learner. My boss hates me.*)

Recognizing what you're saying inside your head is the first step to being able to have more control over it. And having the ability to shift those inaccurate, unhelpful, unsupportive statements to be more accurate, neutral, and supportive is a powerful capability. Without that capability, we tend to be at the mercy of that internal voice and what it tells us about ourselves, our situation, and those around us.

We took a minute just now to listen to that voice, but 99 percent of the time, we don't hear it; it's whispering to us beneath our conscious awareness without us recognizing that it's there. And because it's inside our head, murmuring along like subliminal advertising, we tend to believe what it says, even if it's not true. For example, if that voice in your head tells you, *My people love working for me*, you're probably going to believe it. And that means you won't take the necessary steps to find out how your employees actually feel…and you won't then be motivated to do something about it, if it should turn out that there's a problem. Unless you first recognize your self-talk, and then question it, it's difficult to become neutrally self-aware.

Here are the steps involved in managing your self-talk:

- ➤ Recognize
- ➤ Record
- ➤ Rethink
- ➤ Repeat

Recognize

The first step in managing your self-talk is to "hear" it. Most of the time, as I noted earlier, our little interior commentator runs and runs, and we're not even consciously aware that we're talking to ourselves, much less what exactly it is we're "saying." Until you're aware of this internal monologue, it's impossible to change it. So, first you need to simply recognize what you're saying to yourself. For instance, let's say you're thinking about something you don't want to learn (but have a sneaking suspicion you may really need to learn). You might hear your mental voice saying, *I don't have time to learn how to delegate—I'll just keep doing things myself. I'll do them better anyway.* Or you might find yourself saying surprisingly negative, unhopeful things about your ability to learn: *I'm just bad with numbers that's all there is to it,* or *What's the use I'll never be able to manage people.* Once you start attending to the voice in your head, you may be very surprised at what you're saying to yourself.

Record

Writing down your self-talk, once you recognize what you're saying to yourself, is an important part of being able to change it, particularly if it's something you've said to yourself repeatedly over a long period of time (most of us have a few of these unhelpful "mental tape loops"). Recording your self-talk creates a useful separation between you and your self-talk. When you see it written down, that internal monologue tends to feel less like an intrinsic part of you and more like something you can alter. Let's say you write down that first self-talk statement, above: *I don't have time to learn how to delegate—I'll just keep doing this myself. I'll do it better anyway.* Having written it down, you may see it more objectively, rather than automatically accepting its validity. It's easier to see the inaccuracy and illogic of the things you're saying to yourself once you see them in writing.

The first piece of my own negative self-talk I wrote down, over thirty years ago as a new parent, was, *I'll never be able to juggle work and parenting* (an unfortunately common piece of self-talk for women). My immediate reaction, once I saw it written down, was: *THAT'S what I've been thinking? Yikes. I don't want to say that to myself—I bet it's not even true!* The minute I wrote it down and looked at it, I was able to separate myself from it enough to start questioning its validity.

Once you recognize and record your self-talk, you'll also be better able to look objectively at how this negative interior monologue affects you: perhaps it makes you more likely to abandon goals that are important to you, or to feel cynical or hopeless about the possibility of learning something new.

Rethink

After you've written down a piece of inaccurate, unsupportive self-talk, you can decide how to revise it to be more accurate and helpful. This step is the core of the process. You want to create alternative self-talk that you'll *believe* and that will lead to a more appropriate response. For instance, if you try to substitute self-talk that's falsely positive, like, *Delegating will be a piece of cake*, you simply won't believe it, and therefore it will have no impact on you: you'll just revert to your original unhelpful self-talk. Think about what you could say to yourself instead that's believable and that would create a more useful response. How about something like: *I know it might take a while to learn to delegate well. But if I can transfer some of my responsibilities to my team, I'll be freed up to focus on the most important work and they'll grow and feel more challenged.*

Repeat

Like any habit, managing your self-talk requires repetition. Substituting more hopeful and accurate self-talk for your negative self-talk will be helpful the very first time you do it. *And* you'll need to consciously do it again the next time the voice in your head comes up with a similarly unhelpful statement. And again. This is a process for creating new habits of thought. Whenever you find yourself falling into a pattern of unhelpful self-talk—either overly negative or overly positive—consciously substitute your revised, more realistic and accurate self-talk.

TRY IT

Before we go on to the second step in building neutral self-awareness, I'd like you to do a real practice of shifting your own self-talk from less supportive to more supportive.

Focus on the topic you chose in chapter 3 that you don't want to learn. Write down some of what you're saying to yourself about it.

Circle one piece of the self-talk you've written above that seems particularly unhelpful to you. (For instance, *It will be so frustrating trying to learn this, it's not even worth it.*)

Now rethink that self-talk to be more accurate and believable; write your new, more supportive self-talk. (For instance, *I don't know if it will be frustrating—I haven't really tried it yet.*)

Try saying your revised self-talk to yourself in place of the original self-talk. Do you believe it? If not, rethink it to make it more believable yet still supportive. You'll know you're successful at managing your self-talk when you begin to respond to the situation in a more positive way—when you begin to feel better and to behave differently.

Becoming Your Own Fair Witness

Now we're going to apply your new tool of managing your self-talk in a very specific way, in order to increase your neutral self-awareness. You're going to learn to be a fair witness of yourself. The term "fair witness" comes from a book by Robert Heinlein, *Stranger in a Strange Land*. In it, Heinlein creates a profession called Fair Witness. At one point, a character in the book named Jubal is trying to explain the concept of fair witnessing to the book's protagonist, a man named Michael. Michael is having a hard time understanding, so Jubal calls over a woman who is a Fair Witness, points to a distant house (they're standing outside), and asks, "What color is that house?" She replies, "It appears to be painted white on this side."

That's what Fair Witnesses do, in Heinlein's book: they are trained and then bound by law, when acting in their FW capacity, to speak only from their direct experience. They can't indulge in speculation, cherry-pick the data, say what they hope is true, or avoid looking at what they don't want to be true. In other words, they're proscribed from doing all the things we generally do when thinking about ourselves.

Because fair witnessing means being as objective and accurate as possible, working on becoming a fair witness of yourself is the best way I know to increase your level of neutral self-awareness—and thereby expanding your ability to learn new things well and quickly.

Now, here's the problem with this: the more emotionally attached you are to something, the more difficult it is to be fully objective about it. That means it can be challenging to "fair witness" your own strengths and weaknesses, as well as your feelings about them, since we're generally more emotionally attached to ourselves than to anything else in our lives. I'm sure you've noticed, for example, how much easier it is to see other people's problems clearly and to give them good advice than it is to see your own problems and the best solutions to them.

Remember when we talked about self-deception at the beginning of the chapter? I think of those poor college professors who are actually in the bottom 10 percent of expertise, worse at their job than 90 percent or more of their colleagues, who want so much to believe that they're good at what they do (and perhaps are so afraid that they can't be better than they are now), that they simply can't be fair witnesses about themselves as teachers. That's called emotional attachment.

Fortunately, this rather demanding and often uncomfortable task of becoming your own fair witness can happen in the privacy of your own mind, because it's all about revising your self-talk in a specific way. Here's how it works.

Becoming your own fair witness:

➤ Recognize/record your self-talk about your own current strengths and weaknesses in an area where you want to learn
➤ Then ask yourself, *Is my self-talk accurate?*
➤ Where you're not sure, ask, *What facts do I have about myself in this area?*
➤ Rethink your self-talk to be more accurate, based on your answers

By asking yourself, *Is my self-talk accurate?*, you're beginning to challenge your untested assumptions about yourself. In response to that question, you may find yourself thinking, for instance, *Hmm, I don't really know if that's accurate—it may be just what I hope, or what I think someone in my position ought to be capable of doing.*

If asking the first question causes you to question your initial assumptions, then by next asking, *what facts do I have about myself in this area?*, you're encouraging yourself to be even more neutral and objective in your self-assessment. You're beginning to make the effort—like fair witnesses do—to rely more on real data and observable results (and less on hope and fear) to come to conclusions about yourself.

Here's a practical example. I recently began coaching a senior leader who had been told by someone that he was intimidating. "That's ridiculous," he said to me, clearly upset. "I'm really friendly and approachable!"

"You don't think of yourself as intimidating," I replied. He nodded. "I'd encourage you to look at that assumption for a minute, though," I said. "Is it accurate?"

He started to respond right away, then stopped himself (we had already been working on self-awareness). I saw him start to self-reflect. "I've always told myself I'm an approachable kind of guy," he said slowly, "Not the kind of leader who acts like he wants everybody to defer to him." (The "told myself" was a dead giveaway that he was recognizing his self-talk.)

"So, what actual facts do you have about your behavior in this area?" I asked.

He put his chin in his hand and looked down at the floor—again, reflecting rather than reacting with his previous assumptions. "Well, I do joke around with people, and they seem to like that." He thought for a few moments. "But, you know, I can be pretty blunt when I don't like an idea, or when things aren't going the way I think they should."

"Blunt, meaning…" I said.

He had the grace to look a little abashed. "Well, I can be loud. And dismissive, too. Hmm. I could see that might even be intimidating, given I'm the boss."

Voilà: increased neutral self-awareness.

You can have this same kind of dialogue with yourself—and, as I noted before, it's significantly less embarrassing when there's not another person in the room. Let's give it a shot.

TRY IT

Focus on the topic or skill you chose in chapter 3 that you don't want to learn. Note your self-talk about your current strengths and weaknesses, relative to this area of learning.

Review what you've written and ask, Is it accurate? Circle anything you suspect may not be accurate. (For example, *I don't have a problem admitting when I'm wrong.*)

Now, ask yourself, What facts do I have in this area? (For example, *I can actually think of a number of situations where I was wrong and didn't admit it, or made excuses.*)

Based on your thinking, rethink your self-talk to reflect your more neutral self-awareness. (For example, *It's often difficult for me to admit when I'm wrong.*)

Your conclusions from the activity above may have been surprising to you. You might now see yourself differently than you did a few minutes ago: as having a strength you didn't previously acknowledge or as being less skilled or capable in some area than you assumed.

Managing Your Reactions to What You See

You might also have noticed some "secondary self-talk," interior commentary on your feelings about what you've discovered. For example, if you uncovered an unrecognized capability, you might be saying something to yourself like, *Huh, I guess I have shown that I can make pretty good presentations—that's a relief.* However, if you've started to acknowledge that you're worse at something than you assumed, you may notice some self-talk that reflects the core fear we discussed at the beginning of the chapter. That is, once you realize that you're not very good at something, your self-talk may be asserting that you'll never be able to do it, for instance: *Well, that's embarrassing—I've been acting like I was great at that, when I'll probably never be any good at it.*

You can manage that self-talk, too. Feeling embarrassed, frustrated, nervous, or disappointed is okay, and often inevitable, when we realize we're not as skilled or capable as we thought. If our self-talk stopped at neutral reporting of those feelings (*Well, that's embarrassing*), it would be okay—good even—because it's as useful to be a fair witness about how you feel about your strengths and weaknesses as about the strengths and weaknesses themselves. However, our self-talk often then goes on to predict all kinds of negative outcomes, including the most dire prediction: that we're "fixed" at our current level of capability and can't improve (*I'll probably never be any good at it*). Unfortunately, that voice in our head says all of these things as though they're equally true, so we tend to believe the negative predictions as much as we do the neutral reporting.

You can use the skill you've just learned in this situation, too: you can rethink this secondary self-talk to be more "fair witness"— and therefore more supportive. For example, you could say to yourself, *Hold on, I've gotten better at lots of things. There's a good chance I can get better at this.* Much more accurate, and much more helpful. (We'll talk a lot more about the "self-talk of self-belief" in chapter 7—I just wanted to reassure you now that you don't have to buy your "I'll never improve" self-talk when it arises.)

These are such simple, powerful tools. Most people don't even know they talk to themselves; now you're aware of it and can start to manage that interior monologue to your own benefit.

The Power of a Mirror

Even people who are extremely self-aware can't see themselves entirely clearly, however. For example, we may think we're good at something simply because we've never met anyone who's better at it than we are, or because we don't really know what's involved in being good. Or we might err in the opposite direction: set an unrealistically high bar for "goodness," and therefore think we're worse at something than we actually are. Because it's difficult to be entirely objective about ourselves—especially in areas that are new to us—we also need some outside help in order to be truly accurate and neutral in our self-awareness.

A former business partner of mine used to say, "Feedback is the breakfast, lunch, and dinner of champions," by which he meant that getting input on ourselves is key to success. I agree—as long as we're open to hearing it, and as long as the feedback we're getting is both accurate and well intentioned.

Once you're managing your self-talk to increase your neutral self-awareness, you're already working on the "open to hearing it" part. Taking care of the "accurate and well intentioned" part is what we're going to focus on now.

When you're considering who to ask for feedback about yourself, there are three important things to consider.

Good "sources":

➤ See you clearly
➤ Want the best for you
➤ Are willing to be honest

All three of these qualities are equally important. For example, you might have someone in your life who supports you and is willing to share his honest perceptions of you but doesn't see you clearly. A C-level executive I know who has some significant flaws as a leader generally looks only to his wife and his longtime coach as sources—but unfortunately, neither of them sees him as others do; they don't acknowledge his weaknesses. As a result, he gets a lot of feedback, but it doesn't support him in being more neutrally self-aware.

Another possibility: folks who see you clearly and are willing to be honest, but don't want the best for you. Sadly, such people exist. And while their feedback may be accurate, it's likely to be delivered in a way or in a situation (at a big meeting in front of your boss and all your peers, for instance) that's not geared toward helping you succeed.

Finally, you may know people who see you clearly and have your best interests at heart but aren't willing to be honest with you. We've actually found this to be very common, and I'm sure you have, too. We all have friends and colleagues who know us well and want us to succeed, but when it comes to being honest about our shortcomings and areas of growth...well, they chicken out. Quite often, people will share with me insights they have about another person—a colleague or family member—that would really help that person to see herself more clearly. And when I ask, "Have you shared this with that person?" the most consistent response I get (usually accompanied by a sheepish look) is, "Well, no. I'm not sure she would want to hear it."

People don't share honest feedback with others, for the most part, because they don't know how it's going to be received. You can change this dynamic for yourself: you can become a person to whom it's easy to give even the most difficult feedback. Before I share with you how to do that, I'd like you to pick a couple of possible "sources."

TRY IT

Focus once again on the topic or skill that you don't want to learn. Think of two people who see you clearly in this area (that is, have a balanced and accurate view of your strengths and weaknesses), and who want the best for you.

Setting the Stage for Honesty

Think about the people in your life with whom you are most honest. What makes it possible to tell them difficult or unflattering things about themselves? If you're similar to most people, you're more likely to share tough truths with people who fully take in what you say, without reacting negatively. For instance, imagine that you say to a colleague, "When you didn't get us that information you promised, it made it much harder for us to meet our deadline," and he listens to you without interrupting and then says something like, "I'm really sorry. I didn't realize my info would impact your deadline like that." With an open and non-defensive response like that, you'd be infinitely more likely to continue to be honest with that person. Now imagine instead that his response was something like, "Hey, I was really busy. And besides, I'm not responsible for your deadlines!" I doubt you'd be as honest with that person going forward.

So, if you'd like your selected sources to be honest with you, it's your job to make it as pleasant and rewarding as possible for them to do so. (To take a page from our chapter on aspiration—if people can see the benefits of being honest with you, they're much more likely to want to do it!)

Here's the best way I know to become the kind of person to whom it's easy to give honest feedback—in other words, to take full advantage of your sources so you can have the chance to increase your neutral self-awareness.

When tapping into your sources:

- ➤ Provide context
- ➤ Invite and reassure
- ➤ Listen fully
- ➤ Say thank you

Provide Context

Let your sources know why you're asking them to share their insights with you. This could be as simple as saying something like, "I'm trying to get much more knowledgeable and expert about social media marketing, and I feel as though you see my strengths and weaknesses very clearly in this area. I value your insights, and I know you want to help me improve." Letting others know why you're asking for feedback will generally lower their anxiety significantly. Imagine, by contrast, that you were to just walk up to your source and ask, "How do you think I am at social media marketing?" I can only imagine the resulting storm of self-talk in your source's head (*What's this about? Did I say something I shouldn't have? Should I really be honest? What if my colleague gets upset?* etc., etc.) You can save your sources from all of this speculation by letting them know what you're looking for and why you're asking.

Invite and Reassure

Once you've let your source know why you're looking to her for feedback, ask for it explicitly—and reassure the person that you'll take it well. This might sound like, "I'd really like to know how you see my strengths and weaknesses in this area, and I promise I won't be offended, no matter what you say!" We've found that the main reason people feel uncomfortable sharing tough feedback is concern about negative outcomes: they're worried the receiver will get angry, sad, or defensive, or that it will damage their relationship. Your explicit invitation and reassurance will help to address this key concern, making it much more likely your source will share what she really sees about you.

Listen Fully

After reassuring your source (and next comes the hard part), you have to actually deliver on those reassurances. Even if the other person says something you don't think is true about you, or something that makes you feel really uncomfortable—something that sets off a barrage of justifying, defensive, or argumentative self-talk inside your head—just keep listening. Recognize your unhelpful self-talk, and manage it by saying to yourself, *I really want this person to know I can take in this feedback, so he or she will keep being honest with me.*

If writing down the key points helps you not to blurt out the explanatory or defensive rejoinders running around inside your head, start writing! Get curious about what your source is seeing and why (you'll learn more about how to get curious in the next chapter). Ask questions for clarity; summarize to make sure you understand. Listen deeply, thoroughly, and fully. (If you think you may need more in-depth support for learning to listen well, feel free to refer to some of my other books, where I discuss listening in more depth: the first chapter in *Growing Great Employees* or the final "bonus" chapter in *Leading So People Will Follow.* I see listening as a foundational skill, in learning and in all other arenas, so I talk and write about it a lot.)

Say Thank You

When someone overcomes his own hesitation and is brave enough to tell you both what you're great at and what you're not, that person deserves your thanks. People who give you honest feedback have gone out on an emotional limb for you, and they've invested time and effort articulating their insights in ways that will be helpful to you. In addition to the fact that it's well deserved, there's another reason for thanking your sources: it's really motivating for them. When you sincerely thank people for doing something, they're much more likely to do that thing again. (Back to aspiration—being thanked is a benefit; it will make people want to continue to be honest with you.) By thanking your sources sincerely for their honesty, you're laying the foundation for future honesty—and increasing the chances that you'll be able to use what they tell you to become ever more neutrally self-aware.

TRY IT

Take a few minutes to decide how you'll ask one of your sources for his or her insights about your strengths and weaknesses in the area where you don't yet want to learn (though I hope that's starting to change as you've worked through these last two chapters).

Note the learning topic:
How will you provide context?

How will you invite and reassure?

What self-talk can you use to help assure that you listen fully to what your source says?

Now you have some good, simple tools for building a more accurate perception of your own strengths and weaknesses—for increasing your neutral self-awareness.

Just in case you need another example of the power of neutral self-awareness as a factor in learning and success, consider this: Eric Harter, the CEO of Vesta Technology Solutions, a company based in Louisville, Kentucky, conducted a study of CEOs of health services companies, in order to explore the impact of executive self-awareness on company performance.[3]

Harter studied CEOs of health services companies that showed ten years of positive financial performance (measured by balance sheet results and return on equity) and compared them with their peers at companies with negative financial performance during the same period. He compared all of the CEOs' self-assessments on ten leadership abilities with their subordinates' assessments of them on those same abilities (including, for example, self-confidence and empathy). He found that self-awareness was highest among CEOs of the best-performing companies and lowest for CEOs of the worst-performing companies. The CEOs from the poorest-performing companies had little to no neutral self-awareness: they gave themselves the highest ratings of all the CEOs in the study on seven of the ten leadership abilities, while their employees gave them low ratings on the very same abilities. The high-performing CEOs, on the other hand, saw themselves very much as their employees saw them.

The study completely accords with our experiences over the past twenty-five years as coaches and consultants. When executives have high neutral self-awareness, they are better able to take advantage of their own strengths and to grow in the areas where they need to improve. They are able to approach new learning from a neutral, fact-based sense of their own place on the learning curve relative to that new learning.

Like these high-performing executives, like Michelangelo, and like my friend and client Adam, the clearer you are able to get about where you're starting from as a learner, the easier it will be to learn, and the further you'll be able to go.

Aspiration provides the core fuel that will move you forward into new learning; *neutral self-awareness* allows you to see where you are on the journey. And *curiosity* creates the impulse to dig deeply and understand more.

CHAPTER 6

Endless Curiosity: Not Just Kid Stuff

... When it came to solving the problem of creating a physical structure to support him and his assistants, however, Michelangelo had to rely on his own ingenuity. When he realized that scaffoldings built up from the floor would be both hugely expensive and dangerously unstable, he started to wonder how else he could get his crew up near the ceiling in a way that was reasonably stable and safe. In following his curiosity, he ended up designing an innovative scaffolding structure that consisted of a moveable platform resting on brackets inserted into purpose-made holes in the walls, holes that could be filled in after the work was completed...

Oh Sure, Curiosity...

Curiosity is one of those things—like being strategic or listening—that we talk about a lot, and that we all pretty much say is a good thing... but beyond that, we don't really agree on what it means or how to do it. I've often heard executives say, "I'm deeply curious," but then when I observe their behavior, I realize that they think "being curious" means either wanting to know every detail of the things they're responsible for (which, sadly, generally means that person is micromanaging) or having a deep interest in a couple of things (antique cars, say, or designer footwear).

What people rarely mean, when they say they're curious, is *I'm so fascinated by how things work and what might be possible that I'm completely willing to do what it takes to find out more and become more skilled.* And that, to me, is true curiosity: a deep and abiding *need to understand and master.*

What I've come to see is that even though we give lip service to curiosity, we most often don't act curious. In fact, by the time we get to be adults, there's quite a bit of implicit social pressure *not* to be curious...at least in public. I was just talking to someone the other day about a meeting he had been in the day before, where a colleague was talking about her part of the business, a segment that was new to him. He told me that he really wanted to ask her a couple of questions to find out more, but that he didn't, because, in his words, he "didn't want to look dumb."

So even though we say curiosity is good, we're taught to behave as though it's not. And that's a big problem for us, when it comes to learning new things and thriving in this ever-changing world.

It's Wired In

Even though we're largely socialized out of our curiosity by the time we get to be adults, all functional human beings are born curious. We all come into the world fully equipped with that deep need to understand and master. In fact, John Medina, who I referenced earlier and who has done fascinating exploration into the human brain and its capacity to learn, has this to say, in his book *Brain Rules*, about curiosity in babies and little children:

> Let's look under the hood of an infant's mind, at the engine
> that drives its thinking processes and the motivating fuel

that keeps its intellect running. This fuel consists of a clear, high-octane, unquenchable *need to know* [italics mine]. Babies are born with a deep desire to understand the world around them and an incessant curiosity that compels them to aggressively explore it. This need for explanation is so powerfully stitched into their experience that some scientists describe it as a drive, just as hunger and thirst and sex are drives.[1]

I love this premise so much, that curiosity is a drive in babies just as hunger and thirst are drives for them. It perfectly captures the importance of curiosity to our success as individuals and as a species. Think about it: drives are impulses wired into our very being, beneath the level of conscious choice, because they are key to our survival. If a baby doesn't eat, it dies; if it doesn't drink, it dies. I propose that if a baby isn't curious, it dies, too. Maybe not as quickly, but over time: if a baby doesn't care about figuring out how to move, walk, talk, eat, connect to others, manipulate objects—all skills and knowledge acquired through curiosity—that child will fail to thrive. Throughout our history as humans, the more curious a baby or toddler, the more quickly that little person could learn the skills that would make her a full and contributing member of the tribe.

If you've ever spent much time around babies and small children, you've seen what I'm talking about. Their relentless curiosity is what carries them from total dependence on others at birth to an amazing level of function and independence by the time they've reached school age. If you've watched an eighteen-month-old spend twenty minutes wanting to play the same simple game over and over (building a block tower and knocking it down, for instance)—and getting better and better at it each time—or experienced a three-year-old's endless barrage of "Why...?" and "What if...?" and "How...?" questions, you've seen endless curiosity at work.

So, How Do We Get It Back?

Where do we fall off the curiosity path? And—more important to our discussion here—how can we reengage that endless curiosity that we all had as children and apply it to becoming world-class learners?

If you'll forgive me an analogy, think of curiosity as a fire that burns merrily when we're young. Then, as we get older, it dies down, partly because we don't need it quite so much as when we were babies (or haven't, in previous eras) and partly because society's authority figures—rulers, teachers, parents, and bosses—have largely discouraged it as inefficient and/or insubordinate. But I've found that, for almost everyone, the fire of curiosity hasn't gone out completely, and can be restoked. Here's how it works.

To re-become endlessly curious:

➤ Find your own curiosity "sparks"
➤ Fan the flames with self-talk and action
➤ Feed the fire of curiosity daily

Find your own curiosity "sparks." Almost everyone has things (or even one thing) in their life about which they are truly curious. Those are the places to look for your unextinguished sparks of curiosity. For most of us, hobbies are a great place to start looking for those sparks. Much-loved hobbies are the perfect medium for the expression of curiosity: endeavors that we enjoy so much that we spend time and energy exploring them even though we're not getting paid, and where we don't worry (as much) about whether others will "think we're dumb" if we demonstrate our lack of knowledge. When it comes to our hobbies, we are curious. We want to know more, understand more deeply, get better, and find out how things work and why. A little later in this chapter, we'll work on finding your own curiosity "sparks" and getting better acquainted with them, so you can transfer those sparks to other areas of learning.

Fan the flames with self-talk and action. This second step of reclaiming your childhood curiosity relies first on doing something we've already started to explore: recognizing and managing your self-talk. You'll uncover the messages you're sending yourself that impede your curiosity and replace them with self-talk that supports your curiosity. Then you'll learn how to follow up that revised, more curious self-talk with action designed to satisfy your curiosity. By building curious self-talk and action into areas that you want and need to "understand and master," you can turbocharge your learning dramatically.

Feed the fire of curiosity daily. In this final part of reengaging your childhood need to know, you'll focus on making curiosity something you can draw on every day in order to survive and thrive in a world that's changing faster than we ever thought possible. Making curiosity a daily habit (rather than something occasional that's limited to certain hobbies or topics) is a huge step toward future-proofing yourself: being curious opens you up, makes you resilient and hopeful, and sends you toward the new rather than away from it. It's the ideal response to today's world.

How Endless Curiosity Looks

When I first started working with Deborah Turness, she had been the president of NBC News for less than a year. As I prepared for our initial meeting, I realized that it would be hard to imagine a job with a higher degree of being-thrown-into-the-deep-end of the learning pool than hers. As if being the first woman to run a news network in the U.S. after having spent most of her career in the U.K.

and Europe weren't enough, she'd been tasked with envisioning and leading a successful path to the future for NBC News, a respected and long-successful business (home of *The Today Show, NBC Nightly News,* and *Meet the Press*), in the midst of seismic change. In news—even more quickly than in other parts of the evolving media landscape—consumers are rapidly shifting to digital real-time consumption, and every television news outlet is hard-pressed to figure out how to transform its business models to keep up with consumers' preferences while still making a profit.

My main impressions of Deborah, in that first meeting, were of real intelligence, huge energy, and endless curiosity. She was considering engaging me as her executive coach, and she was fascinated by the process. She had worked with a coach in the U.K., and she wanted to know how our approach was different from and similar to what she had experienced, what we would work on, and how we'd stay connected. She asked me lots of questions. And they weren't standard ticking-off-the-boxes questions either. They were questions like, "How do you know if someone is taking best advantage of the coaching?"—curiosity-based questions that would help her *understand and master.* And she really listened to my responses. When people ask a question out of curiosity, I find they're usually very interested in the answer. For someone like me, who sees curiosity as a necessary driver of real learning, it seemed like an auspicious beginning to our relationship.

Over the months, as we started to work together, I saw Deborah's curiosity applied to every aspect of her job. It made her extremely easy to coach, because when she didn't understand something or know how to do something, she almost always demonstrated that childlike drive to know: she wasn't afraid to ask questions, either with me or with her folks, like "Why did that happen?" or "How could that work better?" or "I wonder if we could...?" And, equally important, she took action to find the answers to her questions.

For example, at one point Deborah asked herself, *How can we help all our journalists get better at operating in this less TV-centric news world?* ("How can we...?" is a great curiosity-based question—we'll talk more about that later in the chapter.) And then she pursued her curious self-talk by asking that question of others, and by starting to experiment with possible answers. One important change that arose from asking that question: Deborah hired a senior person to be the SVP of editorial for all of NBC News, a job that hadn't previously existed. Part of this person's job was to bring the journalists together to learn from one another and to find out what works in this new media landscape, while assuring that they maintain journalistic integrity and have the resources and support they need to succeed.

I've also seen Deborah's curiosity help her weather a variety of crises and reverses, all of them played out very much on the public stage, given the scrutiny to which network news is subjected in the U.S. For example, when she and her boss realized that a very high-profile new hire was operating in ways that were bad for the business, they had to decide—and decide quickly—whether to let the person go. Before making the decision, Deborah quietly gathered information about this executive from a number of people she trusted. And I noticed that she did it with curiosity rather than to support a preexisting assumption: that is, she wasn't trying to build a case against the person, but rather was genuinely trying to find out what had happened and the impact it had had, so that she could make the best decision.

I've noticed another benefit of her curiosity. When she arrived, many of the folks at NBC News, while smart and well intentioned, had been doing things a certain way for a long time, and didn't seem curious about possible alternatives. Many of them, in fact, spent more energy focusing on why the status quo was important rather than on how it might need to change. I've seen that, in many cases, Deborah's curiosity has ignited theirs—more and more people on her wider team are starting to ask, "Why not...?" and "What if...?" and "How can we...?" And that bodes well for the future of the business.

Find Your Curiosity "Sparks"

Before we go on, let me say this: you may already be curious. You may approach every new situation with a bias toward discovering more, understanding more deeply, and figuring out new and better ways of operating in that situation. You may already be insatiably curious about everything that crosses your path. If so, congratulations. If not, let's help you reclaim your birthright of endless curiosity.

I noted earlier that nearly all of us have something that we're curious about in our lives. And I observed that we often lavish our most ardent curiosity on our hobbies. For instance, a woman whose hobby is ballroom dancing might take classes at night, participate in competitions, and watch YouTube videos of world-class dancers. She might also read books about the history of ballroom dancing, compare dancing shoes online to find out which are considered better and why, engage in discussion about which styles of dancing are more elegant or more dashing, and talk to people who are highly skilled in order to learn how they practice and what they've done to overcome obstacles to improvement. In other words, she would explore ballroom dancing in as many ways as are available to her, in order to *understand and master*; she is deeply curious about ballroom dancing.

By identifying those sparks of curiosity that still burn in your own life, you can ignite your curiosity in other areas. That is, by observing what you say to yourself and how you act when you're feeling curious, you can begin to create those same thoughts and actions in other areas where you want to get more curious. Let's explore.

TRY IT

What's a topic about which you're curious? (If you're demonstrating some of the behaviors I noted above around a topic, you're curious about it.)

Reflect on the time you spend exploring this topic: What does that feel like? (For example: exciting, fun, invigorating, challenging, or satisfying.)

What's some of your self-talk about this topic? (For example: *How does that work?* or *I wonder if I could do that?*)

Finally, what do you find yourself doing in response to your self-talk? (For example: reading more, asking more questions, trying some new things, finding a teacher, joining an affinity group.)

There you have it. Now that you know what your own curiosity looks and feels like, you can begin to transfer those "sparks" to new areas about which you may not now feel curious and start to fan the flames of curiosity in order to ignite your learning in those areas.

Fan the Flames of Self-Talk and Action

I don't actually know if toddlers have self-talk. I suspect they just immediately say whatever is in their heads; it's not until we get older that we talk to ourselves about things before or instead of speaking them aloud. In large part, this results from the socialization process most of us go through on the way to adulthood: we learn that it's not socially acceptable to say to someone, "You're skinny and you have a funny nose," as we might have done when we were four—and so we make that comment to ourselves, mentally.

In addition to all the things we think and decide not to say out loud, our adult self-talk is also composed of admonitions and beliefs about ourselves and the world that we've acquired along the way, from parents, teachers, friends, and—these days—the media. Once you start to recognize and manage your self-talk, as we discussed in the previous chapter, you may begin to notice some of this. For example, in my twenties, when I started to become aware of my own self-talk, I noticed myself thinking both helpful and unhelpful things that got passed on to me from others, like "Beautiful women are dumb—don't be beautiful, be smart" (courtesy of my mom, unfortunately), "You can be anything you want to be" (a wonderful contribution from my dad), and "If you talk all the time, you won't find out anything new" (from a wise and acerbic professor at college).

Bringing your self-talk to your conscious awareness, as we explored in the last chapter, allows you to sort the wheat from the chaff: to recognize and retain the self-talk that serves and supports you, and discard or rethink the rest.

That's what I'm encouraging you to do now with the "self-talk of curiosity." When you reflected, above, on your self-talk about the topic where you're curious, you may have surfaced thoughts like:

How does that work?
I wonder if I could do that?
Why does that happen?
How can I find out more?
Why isn't that like this?
I wonder what would happen if I tried this?

You may notice a pattern here: I realized in observing good learners over the years, and working on my own skills as a learner, that curious self-talk most often begins with "Why…?" "How…?" or "I wonder…?" The *need to understand and master* is almost always the driving impulse behind those three sentence starters.

In our work at Proteus, we've also noticed (in ourselves and our clients) what we've come to call "anti-curiosity self-talk." That tends to sound like:

That's boring.
Who cares?
I already knew that.
That doesn't matter.
That's silly.
Whatever, dude.

The pattern here, as you may have noticed, is *disinterest and dismissal*.

As you might already have guessed, your first task in the "fanning the flames" part of reigniting your curiosity is to shift your self-talk from anti-curious to curious in the areas where you want (or need) to learn.

Let's go back to our friend Ron, the librarian from the "Aspiration" chapter who doesn't want to learn to digitize library materials. We'll assume that he has overcome his lack of aspiration by seeing the benefits of learning this new part of his job and envisioning a future where he's experiencing those benefits. Let's also assume that he's gotten much more neutrally self-aware: he knows he's not comfortable with computers and is worried about whether he'll be able to learn the necessary skills—but he also knows that he's deeply knowledgeable about the library and its collection, and very committed to its ongoing success. And he's an organized thinker. In other words, he's clear about his strengths and weaknesses in this new (to him) area of learning.

Now we'll help him reignite his curiosity and apply it to this topic. Ron, it turns out, is reading this book along with you (what a useful coincidence!). He's just done the activity focusing on the topic about which he's curious. For him, that's French wines, specifically the wines of the Rhone Valley. Ron is absolutely fascinated by this topic, and, in fact, he and his wife have even bought a share in a Rhone Valley vineyard. He reads books about wine, gets the feeds of a number of wine blogs, eats at restaurants based on their wine lists, and loves having in-depth conversations with sommeliers and restaurant owners about various vintages. His curiosity about this topic is insatiable. When he reflected on his self-talk regarding wine, he realized that it consisted of questions like, *Why is that vineyard able to produce such wonderful results year after year?* and *How can I continue to improve my palate?* and *I wonder if our vineyard's owners are considering alternatives to cork?*

Then he surfaced what he was saying to himself about the digitization efforts at the library, and realized that it was, indeed, anti-curiosity self-talk, focused primarily on disinterest and dismissal: *This just isn't interesting to me* and *I don't think this is that important* were two of his more unhelpful pieces of self-talk.

So Ron did exactly what I'm about to encourage you to do: he revised his anti-curiosity self-talk about digitization, using his own curious self-talk about wine as a starting point. He revised the two anti-curious statements above to: *I wonder if I could make this more interesting for myself?* and *Why does my boss think this is such a big deal?*

Those might seem like small movements along the path to curiosity—after all, he's only getting curious about whether this topic *might* be worth being curious about—but that's okay. Remember, when you rethink your self-talk, it's critical that the new self-talk be believable by you—and for Ron to go in one jump from *This just isn't interesting to me* to *I'm fascinated—how does this all work?* is probably not realistic. When you're trying to go from spark to bonfire, it can take a little while and some effort to build the blaze.

With Ron's example before you, why don't you take a shot at getting curious about something you want or need to learn.

TRY IT

Pick something about which you're not curious, but that you **need to learn**. (It could be the topic from chapter 3 that you didn't want to learn.)

What's some of your anti-curious (disinterested or dismissive) self-talk about this topic?

Review your own curious self-talk from the previous activity. Use it as a starting point to rethink your self-talk above. Note two believable, curious self-talk questions you could start asking yourself in this area.

Congratulations—you've just transferred your spark of curiosity from one area to another. Now let's help it burn brighter.

Following Self-Talk with Action

When you're genuinely curious about something, the "How," "Why," and "I wonder" questions you're asking yourself demand answers. And you automatically take action to find those answers.

A couple of years ago, I decided I wanted learn how to spin yarn. I was doing a lot of knitting, and when I bought some beautiful yarn at a shop in Asheville, North Carolina, the owner told me that it had been handspun and hand dyed by a local woman. *How cool that would be,* I thought. Eventually I bought a spinning wheel, but it sat gathering dust in my living room for more than a year. Finally, I realized that my aspiration was insufficient. (I had fallen into the trap of confusing mild interest with actual aspiration.) So I ate my own dog food and went through the exercise of identifying the benefits to me of learning to spin and envisioning a future where I would be reaping those benefits. It went something like this: *It would be so gratifying to start with fleece and end up with a garment. So much opportunity for creativity! Such fun to be able to give gifts that are completely handmade.* Then I did some neutral self-awareness building: I have good fine motor coordination and I'm pretty relentless about overcoming obstacles, but I'm also impatient, and I (still) don't like being bad at things.

Armed with aspiration and some self-awareness, I started to get curious. *I wonder if I could learn this from YouTube?* I thought to myself—and followed that curious self-talk by opening my computer, going to YouTube, and searching for "learning to spin yarn." After many videos and numerous failed attempts to do what I saw, I found myself asking another curiosity-based question—*Why isn't this working?* The action that followed was simple reflection, followed by the realization that I probably needed a live teacher to show me what I was doing wrong. I mentioned it to my husband, who got me spinning lessons as a Christmas present. Voilà—I'm now a clumsy novice spinner, getting better with each attempt. (I did notice that my first lesson was much less painful than it would have been without a conscious acceptance on my part of the inevitability of being bad first, but more on that in the next chapter.)

You may have noticed that the actions that followed my curious self-talk were simple efforts designed to answer the questions raised. It's a natural progression: you think, *How . . . ?* or *Why . . . ?* or *I wonder . . . ?* and you want to answer the question. We're built to follow that progression: it's how we've made every human advance in skill or knowledge, from learning how to build a fire to making the latest discoveries in gene therapy. The main thing that gets in the way of that progression from curious self-talk to curious action is a resurgence of anti-curious self-talk. For example, when I wasn't able to learn spinning from watching YouTube videos, and I asked *Why isn't this working?* (good, simple, curiosity-based self-talk), my self-talk response could have been, *Oh, who cares? I've got more important things to think about.* Classic disinterest and dismissal, which would have immediately squelched my impulse to figure out why the You-Tube approach wasn't working and what to do about it.

Remember when we focused on managing your self-talk in the last chapter, and I shared with you the self-talk model of *recognize, record, rethink,* and *repeat?* This is the point in reengaging your curiosity where the "repeat" step is going to come in very handy. As adults, most of us have developed a fairly strong habit of talking ourselves out of following up on our curiosity. I'm sure you've done it yourself: you feel curious about something, and instead of doing something to satisfy that curiosity, you tell yourself it's not important or that you don't really want to know or that you'll look dumb—you revert to old, curiosity-killing self-talk.

When this happens, there are two simple things you can do to set yourself back on the path of curiosity and learning. First, simply go back to your original curious self-talk. In my case, that would have meant saying to myself, *No, I really do want to know why this isn't working.* (It's quite liberating to realize that you can "talk back" to your own unhelpful self-talk, and that you don't have to believe the unhelpful things your inner voice tells you.)

Second, choose follow-up actions that are easy *for you.* For example, in my case, I'm constantly on the Internet, looking for answers to questions or finding out how to do things, so that's always an easy first action for me to take in order to follow my curiosity. For someone else, asking a friend might be an easier and more natural first action. And for another person, just trying something out might be the easiest thing to do first.

I've noticed, for instance, with my client and coachee Deborah, that her first action following curiosity is often to pull some people together, bounce her question off of them, get their responses, and go from there. She's very people-oriented and collaborative, so those next steps are natural for her.

Now that you've got some tools for turning your newly minted curious self-talk into action, let's put them to use.

TRY IT

Review your new-made curious self-talk from the last activity. Note one or two simple (for you) actions you'll take to answer the questions you've raised.

If anti-curious self-talk arises that could keep you from taking those actions, how will you repeat your curious self-talk to allow yourself to keep learning?

Feed the Fire of Curiosity Daily

If you start applying the tools we've been talking about—revising your self-talk from anti-curious to curious and taking action to pursue your curiosity—you'll find that a powerful shift begins to occur inside you. The momentum toward being largely incurious, which for most of us increases throughout our lives, will slow and begin to reverse. More and more often, you'll be sitting in a meeting, riding on the subway, or reading a book and find yourself thinking, *Huh. I wonder if...?* or *Why does that...?* or *How can I...?* That's your natural curiosity reawakening, reigniting.

I'm assuming, since you've read this far, that you want that to happen, that you're seeing your curiosity as an asset and you want to unleash it even further. If so, there's one simple thing you can do to turbocharge your curiosity: create your own personal "curiosity match" and use it every day.

You know how a match works: it's the simplest and most reliable way to start a fire. A curiosity match is a piece of self-talk that works for you to simply and reliably spark your curiosity. Once you've identified your own curiosity match, you can apply it whenever and wherever you like.

Michelangelo had a curiosity match—I talked about it in chapter 3. It was "I am still learning"—*Ancora imparo* in Italian. His biographers tell us that he said it often: as a response to compliments, when approaching a new problem, or in asking others for their knowledge or insight. What a wonderful spark for curiosity! My own curiosity match is, *I'd love to know more about that.* That works for me: it's accurate (I mostly *do* want to know more about things), it encourages me to get as curious as I'd like, and it leads directly to great curiosity-based self-talk and action.

Like all good self-talk, your curiosity match has to be something that's true for you. And it has to be something that will support further curiosity. The easiest way to craft a curiosity match for yourself is to notice something positive that you're already saying to yourself about being curious, and apply it more broadly. Before we leave this ANEW skill, let's build you a really good match that will help reignite your endless curiosity daily.

TRY IT

Think of some topic about which you're very curious. Note some of your positive self-talk about learning this topic. (For example, *I love finding out about this, It's satisfying to know more in this area,* or *I have fun learning about this.*)

Choose one of your statements and revise it to apply more broadly. (For example, *I love finding out about things, It's satisfying to know more,* or *I have fun learning.*)

There you have it: a first draft of your very own, custom-built curiosity match. I encourage you to try it out over the next week or two as you run into topics and skills that are new to you, or in areas where you have lots to learn.

And if it doesn't work—that is, if it doesn't spark your curiosity in these areas—build another "match" and try that one. You're a novice in this area of consciously developing your curiosity, so it's inevitable that you won't be great at the beginning. Nobody (with the possible exception of Mozart) starts out being an expert at anything he or she hasn't done before.

Even though that's true, and even though we all understand rationally that there's no possible way to be good at something you're just starting to learn, our discomfort with being novices is, nonetheless, nearly universal. And that discomfort is the final barrier to becoming a world-class learner. Remember the guy I talked about earlier, who didn't ask questions in a meeting because he didn't want to look dumb? Being willing to "look dumb"—to make mistakes, to be clumsy, to not know—is the final frontier in becoming a master of mastery, and that's where we're going next.

CHAPTER 7

Willingness to Be Bad First:
The Trap of Competence

...The work went slowly at first, both because Michelangelo was inexperienced with the medium and because the unusual size and configuration of the surface created unique problems. For example, he discovered about a third of the way through the project that the need to keep such large areas moist enough to paint meant the plaster would often get moldy before it dried. He ripped out a huge area of the work that had been damaged by mold, and asked one of his assistants, Jacopo Torni, known as L'Indaco, an experienced fresco painter, for a solution. L'Indaco created a more mold-resistant plaster formula, which Michelangelo used for the remainder of the job (and which, in fact, subsequently became the standard for Italian fresco-painting)...

We Hate This

By the time we get to be adults, we're good at some stuff. And we really love that. Remember in chapter 2, when I talked about our inborn human drive toward mastery? We want deeply to be good at things. Nearly everyone wants to feel expert at something, and we take great pride in relying on and demonstrating our expertise. I've discovered, for instance, that you can be at a party and never have to say anything about yourself at all if you simply ask other people questions about stuff they're interested in and are expert at doing (or think they are). As we've discussed, there's a very good side to this drive toward mastery—it has kept the human race moving forward in every realm of skill and knowledge since the dawn of time.

The dark side of this drive of ours is that we want so much to be good, and we see being good at things as such a valuable accomplishment and so central to our adult identity, that it really upsets us to be not-good. Most of us, as adults, deeply dislike and strongly resist the novice state, that clumsy, helpless feeling of not understanding and not being able to do something. To make this more personal, think of the last time you were in this situation. Perhaps someone was showing you a complex process at work that was new to you and that you needed to use in your job. Or maybe you had to learn a program (like our friend Ron, the librarian) to do a task you'd always done manually. Perhaps your boss said to you, "We have to find new ways to market our product. I know you haven't worked on this before, but I'm assigning it to you..." If you reflect on how you felt as you were trying to learn the new skill: making mistakes, having to do things over, not getting why something wasn't working and not even knowing what to ask to get clear—I suspect you felt some combination of embarrassment, frustration, boredom, anxiety, and impatience. It's the uncomfortable emotional soup most of us find ourselves in when we're required to acquire a new skill.

As I noted in chapter 1, it used to be much, much more possible to go through life without having to confront and move past this resistance to novice-ness as an adult. Until forty or fifty years ago, most people learned the skills and knowledge they needed for their job or career as young people, and then just kept doing that throughout their lives, perhaps occasionally making slight changes or improvements. And even those few people who had to expand their knowledge base more dramatically did so gradually, over many years. For instance, a young man might come into his father's business directly out of school at age sixteen; by the time the father retired or died twenty-five years later, the now-middle-aged son had probably learned enough over all those years to take over the business.

Now, unless you can somehow create for yourself a magical little nineteenth-century job universe that stays the same throughout your working life, you're going to have to go back to being a novice over and over and over again as the expansion of knowledge continues to accelerate, and the capabilities and careers enabled by that new knowledge multiply with mind-numbing rapidity.

In other words—though you may be tired of hearing me say it by now—getting good at being bad first is the most essential and powerful future-proofing tool you can have. So let's talk about how to do it.

Expert at Being Novices

In the early 2000s, a guy named Peter Skillman invented a collaboration exercise that has come to be called the Marshmallow Challenge. Here's how it works: a group of four people are given twenty pieces of spaghetti, a meter of tape, a meter of string, and a marshmallow. They have eighteen minutes to create the tallest freestanding structure possible that will support the marshmallow. After doing this exercise with more than five hundred people over a five-year period, here's what he discovered. Groups of engineers and architects did very well, and groups of business school students consistently did very poorly. No big surprises there. But what group did the best, you might ask, in terms of completing the tallest structures within the allotted time?

Kindergarteners.

That's right. Five- and six-year-olds consistently outperformed business school students, engineers, and even architects in doing this activity. While looking for answers about why this should be so, Skillman noticed three things. First, the kids didn't waste time on "status transactions," that is, deciding who should lead the effort—they just started building. Second, they tried lots of things that ended up not working, rather than trying to just do one thing that would be "right." Finally, they asked for more spaghetti—not a single adult group asked for more materials.

Skillman and others have used this experiment to understand what children can teach us about the importance of collaboration and prototyping in innovation. I looked at the outcome through a different lens: rather than focusing on what the kids did that yielded better results, I started thinking about *why* they behaved differently in the first place. And it occurred to me that everything they did—just getting in and messing around versus worrying about who was the most expert; trying a bunch of different things versus trying to get it right the first time; breaking the (nonexistent, as it turned out) rules by asking for more material—all of these behaviors were possible because they weren't worried about being bad first. As it turns out, someone else noticed the same thing. In her book, *The Up Side of Down: Why Failing Well Is the Key to Success,* Megan McArdle noted that, "The engineers had years of schooling and work experience to teach them how to build sound structures. But the kindergartners had something even more powerful: they were not afraid of failure. By trying and failing, they learned what didn't work—which, it turned out, was all the knowledge they needed to figure out what did."[1]

Just as most little children are much better than most adults at being curious, they are also better at being novices. It's what they're used to, every moment of the day. The world is new to them, and they're figuring it out—they don't put the expectation on themselves that they have to be experts, to know everything already. At the same time, they believe that they'll be able to get better (at least those who have been raised in reasonably loving, non-punitive households), because their entire life to date has been an unbroken string of getting better at things. Here's a kid's world: *I didn't know how to talk; now I do. I didn't know how to put on my clothes; now I do. I didn't know how to catch a ball, ride a bike, sing a song, cut with scissors, count to twenty, close the door, remember my colors; now I do.*

And because they're accepting not-knowing and believing they'll get better, rather than taking up their mental energy with being embarrassed about being not-good and worrying about whether they'll be able to get better, they have the mental bandwidth to use the related knowledge they already have to speed up their learning process. (For example, lots of the kids' marshmallow structures looked like things they were already familiar with: animals, spiders, houses.)

Adults who retain their ability to be novices, their willingness to be bad first, take the same approach. Michelangelo acknowledged not only to himself, but to those around him, that he didn't consider himself a painter, and had only a theoretical basis in fresco—that he was "not-good" at the core skills required. At the same time, he had deep faith in his ability to learn the needed skills—as he noted in a letter to a former student, "Faith in oneself is the best and safest course." And once he was engaged in the project, he drew upon all his related skills and experience as a sculptor, anatomist, and architect to speed his learning.

With that as the blueprint, here's how to reclaim your ability to be an excellent novice.

To become willing to be bad first:

➤ Fully accept being not-good
➤ Believe in your ability to get good
➤ "Bridge" from what you're already good at

And, as you might have suspected, our willingness (or unwillingness) to be bad first lives mostly in the same place as do our neutral self-awareness and endless curiosity: it's all about how you talk to yourself. So in this chapter, you'll learn to take your newly honed skills in managing your self-talk and apply them to becoming great at being bad.

Fully accept being not-good. When we have to do something new, especially in front of others, and we make some inevitable mistakes, our self-talk tends to go something like this: *Oh my god, I'm such a loser—I hope nobody saw me do that… I'll just say I did it on purpose. This is awful. I hate it. Now I look like an idiot.* Not at all helpful and deeply uncomfortable. In this chapter, we'll focus on transforming our enormously unproductive self-talk in these situations into accurate, believable self-talk organized around the understanding that being bad at things that you're doing for the first time is acceptable and, in fact, inevitable.

Believe in your ability to get good. Once you're no longer resisting your initial "badness," you need to assert to yourself that you're capable of moving beyond that novice state, of getting good at whatever it is you're trying to learn. Doing this (again, it lives in your self-talk) allows you to build on your initial acceptance of your novice state to catalyze forward movement into learning. Fortunately, almost everyone has a lifetime of getting better at things to reference in support of this. You'll learn how to balance your new "acceptance of not-good" self-talk with "self-belief" self-talk—so that, like the kindergarteners in the Marshmallow Challenge, your mind and emotions are free to solve the learning challenges before you.

Bridge from what you're already good at. With this more realistic and supportive self-talk in place, you'll be better able to access and use any related skills and knowledge that may already be in your experience set, applying what you now know to what you're just beginning to learn. We'll focus on how to build this "bridge" from your existing knowledge and skills, while avoiding the trap of thinking new things are more like what you already know than they really are. In fact, you can use your newly enhanced curiosity to keep yourself out of that trap—and I'll show you how.

How Willingness to Be Bad First Looks

The first time I spoke with Courteney Monroe, I was surprised and impressed at her degree of openness to the novice state. Courteney had just been promoted to CEO of the National Geographic Channels US, and she was telling me that since she'd never been a CEO, she knew she had a lot to learn. She said it without hesitation or embarrassment, as a simple reality. "I've never reported to a board of directors," she noted, "and I've never run business functions that I haven't had experience doing myself. I'm sure I'll make mistakes—and I want to figure it all out as quickly as possible."

As we talked, I thought to myself: *She's already accepting being not-good, and she has faith in her ability to get better. The ideal starting point.*

And it was. Courteney and I ended up working together with her team to create clear vision and strategy for the organization, and then she engaged me as her executive coach. Throughout our time together, I've noticed again and again her unusual ability to accept being bad first. For example, I've noticed that when she talks with someone who works for her in an area with which she's not familiar, she has no hesitation about asking the person "novice" questions. In fact, she'll say, "I haven't done that before; can you walk me through how that works?" Or even, "I don't understand what you're saying—can you explain it another way?" She doesn't come across as embarrassed or apologetic, because she isn't. I know what her self-talk is in these situations, because we've talked about it. It's very accepting: *I need to learn this, and I don't know it. How would I? I've never run program production (or finance, or IT) before.*

Her balancing self-talk, of belief in herself, sometimes needs a little adjustment (as is true of most of us), but because she has so little resistance to being a novice, she's been able to quickly take in and integrate the feedback I've offered to help her in that realm. The place where I've most noticed the power of having that balance is in the way Courteney has learned to deal with her board. As soon as she started balancing her *I'm going to be bad at reporting to a board to begin with* self-talk with *And I know I'll learn how to do it well, and pretty quickly*—she did. Over a remarkably short period of time, she was able to understand each of her key board members and build strong relationships with them that balanced diplomacy and flexibility with clarity and firmness.

I've also enjoyed seeing how she's been able to "bridge" from her previous jobs as head of marketing (at HBO, and then at the Nat Geo Channels). She realized that her skills in leading people, managing a P&L, and understanding and communicating with consumers in a compelling way were all largely transferable—and then she got curious about how those skills would need to be applied differently in this new role. That's the essence of good bridging: identifying what you already know that can be applied to make your new learning faster or easier, without assuming that what you've known or done before is exactly like what you're learning now.

It's been fascinating watching the impact of Courteney's approach on her team and her board as well. They see her as open, confident, non-defensive, and a quick study. Because she doesn't pretend that she knows things she doesn't know, her team trusts her—and they know it's okay to come to her with things *they* don't know as well. I'm pointing this out partly because it seems counterintuitive; many of the executives I've coached over the years have resisted the idea of "being bad first" because they're afraid their employees won't respect them if they make their ignorance or novice-ness public. My experience, though, is that what's happening in response to Courteney is the norm. When an executive is honest about what he doesn't know, and then makes an effort to acquire that knowledge as quickly as possible, most employees are impressed with that person's openness, bravery, and confidence, and want to support his success. (Of course, this assumes that the executive isn't a novice at *everything* required to do the job—most employees expect that their boss will have most of the necessary skills and knowledge. They don't, however, expect the boss to know everything—and in fact most people find it disingenuous and deeply irritating when their bosses pretend that they're expert in every area.)

I've also seen that Courteney's board members appreciate the way she has invited their insights and experience, rather than trying to act as though she were an expert at being a CEO. And as they've seen her take good advantage of those insights to grow into her position, it's deepened their faith in her ability to run the business well. I also see that her openness to learning gives them a specific confidence that, in this era of especially radical and unpredictable change in the media industry, she'll be able to see and embrace the "new" quickly enough to keep the business moving in the right direction.

Accepting Being Not-Good

As I noted earlier, the core of willingness to be bad first lies in managing your self-talk. If you actually stop and listen to what you're saying to yourself as you're trying to learn something new, you'll notice that the vast majority of it focuses on resisting and bad-mouthing (bad-minding?) yourself about your novice state. For example: *Aagh! I'm so clumsy/stupid/slow! Why can't I figure this out/ do this right/get it together?* Not only does this not help us learn, it gets in the way of our learning to a fairly dramatic extent. When we talk to ourselves like that, we feel embarrassed, helpless, silly, awkward, anxious—maybe even depressed or hopeless. And those feelings tend to lead to even worse, less helpful self-talk—the kind of insidious self-talk that predicts failure. (*I'm such an idiot. Why do I even try? I'll never be able to learn this . . . or anything!*) In fact, our "non-acceptance" mental monologue generates so much emotional and mental static inside us in the form of negative feelings and a spiral of ever-worsening self-talk that it leaves very little of our brain free to focus on learning whatever is in front of us.

Shifting your resistant and self-castigating self-talk into the self-talk of acceptance can create an immediate positive shift in your emotions and a remarkable sense of mental clarity.

Whenever I'm trying to understand and develop a new way of approaching something, I always use myself as a guinea pig. As I've been developing the ANEW model over the past few years, I've made efforts in a variety of areas to heighten my aspiration, increase my neutral self-awareness, engage my curiosity, and—hardest for me—be willing to be bad first. As I mentioned in the last chapter, I've been learning to spin yarn, partly as a way to explore and practice my ANEW skills. Before my first lesson, I realized this was a great opportunity to practice the self-talk of acceptance. I consciously said to myself, *I'm going to be bad at this for a while, because I've never done it before. That's just how it is.* It felt almost like setting down a physical weight. Just acknowledging and accepting the reality of my novice-ness made me feel immediately less pressured, more capable, and hopeful.

And then something very exciting happened. Because I was accepting that I simply wouldn't be good at this first lesson, I found myself behaving very differently than I had in the past in other "first lesson" situations. I had nothing to prove to the teacher or myself, and so I could calmly watch him, try doing what he suggested, notice what wasn't working, ask him what to do differently, and try it again. By the end of the hour I had the basics, and my teacher,

Jamie, actually said, "Wow, you're learning this really quickly." I told him about "accepting being bad first," and he nodded. "That's so true," he said. "I was trying to teach someone recently who was a master weaver, and who thought because of that she should be good at spinning right away. She was so frustrated and impatient when she didn't get it immediately. I kept saying, 'It's okay, you're just starting out, it will get easier.' But it was almost like it didn't penetrate. She just kept getting more unhappy with herself—she actually got worse instead of better. By the end of the lesson, she was completely frazzled and even I was feeling frustrated."

Exactly. When we're faced with new skills or knowledge, and we talk to ourselves in the common, negative ways, our I'm-a-loser-and-I-shouldn't-be-bad-at-this self-talk becomes a self-fulfilling prophecy. Our minds roil with unhelpful negative messages; we start feeling afraid or angry or embarrassed; and our receptors for new information and sensation close down. We become less and less able to learn, which kicks our negative self-talk into even higher gear (*I really am a loser and I'll* never *get this*).

Let's stop the madness.

You've already started learning and practicing the skill of managing your self-talk, and of becoming a fair witness in the service of increasing your neutral self-awareness. You can apply both of those new capabilities to this challenge.

Here's how I did it in preparation for my first spinning lesson. I **recognized** my "anti-being bad" self-talk about it, which was: *This is going to be frustrating. I hate not being able to do things. I hope I don't suck at this too much.* I **recorded** it by writing it down on a piece of paper. As I reviewed it and made the effort to be as fair witness about the situation as possible, I was able to **rethink** my self-talk to be: *I'm going to be bad at this for a while, because I've never done it before. That's just how it is.*

I noticed Courteney Monroe did the same thing before her first board presentation. She told me that she initially recognized her self-talk as being along the lines of, *Oh my god, I hope I don't screw this up and look completely clueless.* And she changed it to, *I've never done this before, so I know I've got a lot to learn about how to do it well. And they know this is my first board meeting.*

Now it's your turn.

TRY IT

Pick a new area of learning where you are worried about being or looking incompetent. (It could be either of your topics from chapter 3, or another area in which you notice your resistance to "being bad.")

What's some of your "anti-being bad" self-talk about this topic?

Review the self-talk above through your fair witness lens. Incorporating what you now know about the inevitability of novice-ness in a new area, create new, accurate self-talk that allows you to accept being bad first.

If you're like most people I know, you'll definitely have to repeat this one—our negative self-talk about being bad is particularly sticky and insidious. I found that I had to remind myself that, *I'm going to be bad at this for a while, because I've never done it before. That's just how it is,* many times before and during that first spinning lesson, and I'm sure Courteney had to repeat her pre-board meeting "acceptance" self-talk as well. By the way, she told me that when she accepted her board-presentation novice-ness, she experienced the same feelings of relief and hopefulness that I had in approaching my first spinning lesson, and as a result she was much more effective in both her preparation and her delivery than she would have been otherwise.

Believe in Your Ability to Get Good

Too often, even if we are able to shift our initial self-talk when confronted with new learning to some form of accepting not-good, like *I'm bad at this right now, and that's the nature of learning something new,* the self-talk that tends to follow immediately is, *And I'm going to be bad at it forever. I'll never get any better.* This goes back to that phenomenon we looked at in chapter 5: the fact that it's often hard for people to be accurate about their current weaknesses because they don't believe they'll be able to improve.

In order to explode that very pernicious belief (which Carol Dweck has termed "fixed mindset"), you need only to look at your own life in a fair witness way. If you review your life objectively, you'll see that you've gotten better at literally thousands of things. Think about what you were able to do when you were five years old; think of all the things you can do now. All human beings can learn and grow. Period. So when that voice in your head starts to predict that not only will you be bad first, you'll be bad *always,* you can shift that self-talk to assert, completely accurately, that *I've gotten good at lots of things in my life, and I'll be able to get better at this.*

You can then make your self-talk of self-belief even more powerful by acknowledging specific things that you've learned that are like this new thing you're attempting, or qualities in yourself that you know make you a particularly good learner. For instance, my balancing self-talk in approaching my first spinning lesson was, *I'm sure I can learn this. I've gotten really good at other crafty things over the past few years, and I'm good at getting curious and figuring out what's not working when I'm faced with something new.* Courteney's balancing self-talk was, *I know I'll quickly get better at reporting to a board. I'm a good learner, and I'll be open to all the cues I get about how to deal with them effectively.*

Now you get to create this second "balancing" self-talk statement to use in approaching your new learning.

TRY IT

Review the "accepting not-good" self-talk you created in the previous activity.

Now create an accurate, simple self-talk statement that reflects your belief in your ability to get good in this area over time. (Acknowledge your history of learning similar skills or your strengths as a learner to make your self-talk even more personal and powerful.)

Leveraging Your Internal Fair Witness

Your ability to be a fair witness is key to creating balanced self-talk as you approach new learning. Remember: fair witnesses report, as objectively and accurately as possible, based on their direct experience. I submit to you that your direct experience (and mine, and nearly everyone's) is that (1) people are not good at things when they first start learning them and (2) each of us has the capability to get significantly better at most things over time.

Are we agreed?

Then, when your mind starts throwing self-talk at you that calls into question these basic truths (i.e., *It's unacceptable to be bad! I bet so-and-so wasn't bad when he started out! Managers are supposed to know everything! I'll never be able to learn this!*), you can go right back to the fair witness approach we discussed in chapter 5, and ask:

➤ Is my self-talk accurate?
➤ What facts do I have in this area to support or refute it?

If you ask yourself those questions, and really try to be objective in your answers, I'm pretty sure you'll come out on the side of the angels. And you can make up your own variations of these "fair witness" questions as well. One of my favorites—when I recognize that my interior voice is either rejecting the truth of having to be bad first or promoting the idea that I'll never get better at something—is simply to ask myself, *Really? Is that even true?* It's like splashing my mind with cold water—bracing and energizing at the same time. And it usually cuts right through the unhelpful and unsupportive BS my mind is blathering on about, and allows me to tell myself things that are more accurate and hopeful.

Bridge from What You Already Know

As I said earlier, most adults are good at a bunch of things. So most of us, when we're approaching learning something new, have done some related learning at some point. This is true even when the learning seems to you entirely different from anything you've ever done. For example, someone I know was offered a job, a few years ago, as head of the new social media marketing effort for a non-profit in her city. Her first reaction was, *Why would they want me? I know nothing about social media.* But the organization was actually seeing related expertise that she wasn't seeing. They knew that she was an educator who understood how to introduce others to new ideas, that she was an artist and would look at their communication with a creative eye, and that she had experience building community with a wide variety of people. They felt she could apply all of this expertise in helping them explore and create a strategy for using social media as a means of reaching and engaging their target audience.

On the other hand, I've often seen people go too far in the

other direction, and assume that new learning is *exactly* like what they already know. I spent many years working with someone who unconsciously used this approach to hide her fear of being bad. For example, at one point (this was many years ago, when our business was quite small), we were planning to start using accounting software, rather than doing our books manually on Excel spreadsheets. As we were reviewing a demo of the software, she said, somewhat dismissively, "Oh, this is just like what I've been doing." I looked at her, puzzled. "Really?" I responded. "I don't know much about accounting, but it seems quite different to me." "No," she assured me, "it's pretty much the same."

Sadly, it took our accountant months to convince her that it was, indeed, different, so that she could actually take advantage of having the software in order to simplify and improve our approach.

In other words, using this tactic of "bridging" in the service of being bad first requires a kind of Goldilocks approach: not too little and not too much, but just right. That is, you don't want to either underestimate or overestimate the relevance of previous learning when you're approaching a new area of skill or knowledge. Your biggest ally in finding that sweet spot is your curiosity. Instead of asserting that something you know is or isn't like the new thing you want to learn, get curious and ask yourself whether or not they are alike, and if so, how.

For example, instead of telling herself that reporting to the board was nothing like anything she'd ever done before (which would have been unnecessarily scary, and not accurate), Courteney asked herself, *I wonder what skills I have that are related to what I'll need to learn in order to report successfully to the board?* What immediately came to mind was that she had a lot of experience presenting; she knew how to build a business case for change; and she knew how to elicit and be open to feedback (from years of presenting to and collaborating with groups as a marketing professional). Then she asked herself a second curious question, *How are those existing skills similar to and different from what will be required in this new situation?* Asking and then reflecting on that question gave her a lot of great information on which to base her preparation for interacting with her board. For example, she realized that simply having learned to be comfortable presenting to groups was going to be a big advantage, and one she could build on in this situation.

At the same time, she saw there was at least one new skill she'd need in dealing with her board: managing the conversation with, in effect, a room full of bosses. She realized it had been much easier, in most of her previous presentations, to simply ask for questions at the end or at specific times during the presentation, but that she was going to have to learn how to have more of a give-and-take with the board without being thrown off track, and help to bring them to consensus or agreement on next steps. As she got curious, she understood that this new responsibility wasn't just going to require good presentation skills, it would require group facilitation skills, along with a much deeper understanding of her whole business than she had previously had to have.

My colleagues at Proteus and I have found over the years, especially in coaching situations, that if we can help our clients to ask the two curiosity-based questions that Courteney asked herself when entering into an important learning situation—a new, bigger job; increased responsibilities; developing an area or offer that's new to the organization—they're much more likely to understand how they can use their existing skills and knowledge well in the new area. (And since we've already worked with them to create good, balanced self-talk, they actually have the mental clarity and emotional bandwidth they need to build from what they know.)

Let's apply this final tactic to your own be bad first challenge.

TRY IT

As you think about the learning topic for which you now have supportive, accurate self-talk that balances accepting not-good with self-belief, ask yourself: *I wonder what skills or knowledge I already have that are related to this new topic?*

Select the skill or expertise you believe is most relevant, and ask yourself: *How is this similar to and different from what will be required in the new situation?*

Your Toolkit Is Full

That's it. You now have the four basic ANEW tools you need in order to thrive through change, and to acquire new skills and knowledge at the pace required in today's world. You've learned the basics of how to make yourself *aspire* to learn the things you need to learn; you know how to become more *neutrally self-aware*—more objective and accurate about your strengths and weaknesses as you approach new learning; you've learned some simple secrets for reengaging your own *endless curiosity*. And now you also know the most important skill for new learning: how to accept and move through the inevitable necessity of *being bad first*.

You, dear reader, have the core of what you need in order to become a master of mastery. Before we part company, though, I want to provide you with even more support along the way. First, I want to inoculate you against your own particular anti-learning demons—do some mastery troubleshooting, if you will—and then I want to work with you to bring together all the activities you've done throughout the book: to apply the ANEW skills to a learning challenge that's really important to you.

First, let's slay some of your dragons...

CHAPTER 8

Slaying Your Personal Dragons: On the Road to Mastery

> If people knew how hard I worked to get my mastery, it wouldn't seem so wonderful at all.
>
> —Michelangelo

If what you've read so far makes sense to you, and you've decided you need to become a high-payoff, Michelangelo-style learner, then you're now at the point where the rubber meets the road. Even though you've had lots of opportunities along the way to try out all the ANEW skills, that was primarily to familiarize you with what they are and how they work. Now, if you really want to get good at this stuff, you'll have to use your ANEW skills to build your ANEW skills.

After that last sentence, you may feel a bit like you're in an echo chamber, so let me explain. If you're serious about becoming a world-class learner, you need to approach it in the same way you would learning any other skill: you need to ramp up your *aspiration* to learn the ANEW skills, get *neutrally self-aware* about where you're starting from in learning them, engage your *endless curiosity* about them—and be *willing to be bad first* at them.

If you're up for that, these last two chapters are designed to speed you on your way. In this chapter, I'll be offering answers to the most common questions we've heard from our clients (and ourselves) in teaching and learning these skills—think of it as a helping hand over the roughest of the rough spots. In the next and final chapter, I'll be giving you a chance to work through all the skills in a real-life, high-importance learning situation of your choosing.

As Michelangelo Says...

...this stuff is not easy. I've been consciously working on becoming a better learner for more than twenty years, and there are days when it's still difficult for me. Over the past few months, for instance, I've had to work hard at ramping up my aspiration to learn in three different areas that are new to me and key to my success right now (e-learning, podcasting, and selling licensed training, in case you're curious), and I've encountered significant internal resistance from myself along the way in all three areas.

But I've found it's totally worth both the effort and any attendant frustration and irritation. Every time I overcome my initial resistance and get traction in a new learning area—when I begin wanting to learn the topic, get clear on where I'm starting from, engage my curiosity, and accept my novice-ness—it's like breaking through an almost physical barrier. I suddenly feel more confident, energized, capable, clear: it feels as though all of my mental and emotional energy are now available to me and directed toward mastery. At that point, the learning process gets liberating, fun, and extremely productive.

What We've Learned Along the Way

Like any good FAQ, the following is organized by topic to make it easier to find what you need. You'll see questions and answers about each of the four ANEW skills, and then a final group about overall difficulties or confusions people have had in working with the model. (And if you run into other difficulties or questions, please let us know at connect@proteus-international.com, for inclusion in future FAQs.)

Aspiration

Q: But what if I just really don't want to learn something?
If it's something you actually don't need to learn, don't burn up your mental and emotional energy trying to find and build your aspiration. Turn your attention to those things you do need to learn. Be careful, though: it's easy to convince yourself that you don't need to learn something simply because you don't want to learn it.

Try to look at the situation through your "fair witness" lens. Put aside, for a moment, the question of whether or not you want to learn the skill in question, and simply focus on how important it is for you to have this capability. Will not having this skill be a career limiter for you? Will it be significantly more difficult to reach any of your important goals if you don't have this skill? If the answer to either of these questions is "yes" (and especially if the answer to both of them is yes), then it's worth your while to find the aspiration you'll need to learn the skill.

If you decide you do need to learn it, as you start to work on ramping up your aspiration, you'll already be a step ahead; by answering the questions above, you will have already begun to define the personal benefits of learning it. You will have determined that, by acquiring this capability, you'll be opening up possibilities to advance your career and/or reach an important goal.

I recently went through this process in one of the areas I mentioned above, podcasting. When we were starting to think about how to market *Be Bad First*, my wonderful digital publicist, Rusty

Shelton, told me that he and his team had been seeing a strong positive impact on awareness and sales for authors who did regular podcasts. I really didn't want to do it, initially, and my not-wanting-to-do-it self-talk was completely predictable and standard: I focused on all the things that might be hard about podcasting (it will take too much time, I don't want to have to think of people to interview, we'd have to figure out how to make it cool, etc., etc.). Rusty, wisely, stopped talking about it...for a while. The next time he brought it up, at our launch meeting for the book, I thought to myself (grumpily, I might add), *Okay, okay, I guess I'm going to have to do this. It sounds like it's going to be significantly harder to achieve our goals for* Be Bad First *if I don't get into podcasting. Damn.*

And once I realized that, I began the process of doing exactly what I'm encouraging you to do. I shifted my focus away from all the obstacles and difficulties, and instead identified some benefits of doing podcasting that were meaningful to me personally (i.e., getting out the word about the book and having a new way of connecting with people to offer them practical help). Then I envisioned a future where I could reap those benefits. (Note: my visioning was very much helped by listening to a great podcast series called *The $100 MBA Show* by Omar Zenhom—listening to his quick, practical, fun, business-focused podcasts, I started to see how I could podcast in a way that would resonate for me.)

Q: Sometimes I'm clear on the benefits of learning something, but I still can't get myself to do it. Like exercise. Or Twitter. What do I do then?

Being clear on the *theoretical* benefits of something and feeling that something will be *personally* beneficial to you are two very different things. Exercise is a great example. You would have to have been living under a really big rock for the past twenty or thirty years not to know that regular exercise is good for you: that it keeps your heart and respiratory system healthy, helps manage your weight, gets you strong, is good for your bones, lowers stress, improves your balance, makes your brain work better, and so on. But unless one or more of those things are really important to you...you won't exercise.

When I started exercising regularly, it wasn't for any of the reasons above. The benefits that engaged my aspiration? I wanted to keep up with my sister, and I wanted to read.

Some explanation: in the early 2000s, my sister lost a good deal of weight and began exercising, and she was clearly happier, more energetic—and looked great. I admire her, plus I'm very competitive, so the idea of looking and feeling as good as she did was very motivating to me. As for the reading: I watched someone reading a magazine while he was using an elliptical trainer, and I realized that if I spent half an hour on the elliptical trainer a few times a week, I'd have the perfect excuse to spend that time reading whatever I wanted. As a busy entrepreneur with two teenage kids, the idea of having some uninterrupted reading time was hugely appealing.

In other words, when you're trying to increase your aspiration so that you can learn something, don't just look at the "standard" benefits of learning that thing. Look for benefits that resonate for you, personally—and perhaps for no one else. (I may well be the only person in the world who started exercising in order to be able to read more.)

Q: Trying to get myself to want to do something seems fake. Shouldn't I just go for what I'm passionate about?

If only pursuing the things you're "naturally" passionate about gives you the kind of life you want, then have at it. However, most of us discover that in order to thrive in this modern world and create the success we want for ourselves, we need to cultivate new passions— sometimes for things in which we haven't previously been interested.

But let's explore this idea of real versus fake passion a little more deeply, because there can be a very subtle resistance to new learning embedded in that distinction. Recently, I was coaching an executive who said something very similar to our question here. He had just gotten some pretty strong feedback that he needed to get better at building relationships with his peers and direct reports, and he was telling me that he thought it would be "fake" to do that when he didn't really want to.

"It's just not me," he said. "I'm not a relationship guy."

"Is there anything else you've had to learn in your career that you didn't really want to?" I asked.

"Sure, lots of things," he responded.

"And those weren't fake because..." I prodded.

"Well, they were job skills. I needed to learn them," he answered. Then he paused. "Aah," he said. A longer pause, then he smiled and shook his head. "So, me saying, 'This just isn't me' is nothing more than my rationale for not doing it. Got it." As soon as he saw what he was doing, we were able to start looking for the benefits to him of learning to build better relationships. (And interestingly, he realized that "finding the benefits" was the way he'd gotten himself to acquire other job skills that he wasn't thrilled about having to learn in the past.)

So, be a fair witness: if you're telling yourself that learning to do something differently is "fake" or "inauthentic," it may simply be a convenient way of rationalizing your lack of aspiration.

Q: Learning something complex often requires learning lots of subskills. Do I have to aspire to learn each of those?
The colleague and friend who asked me this question is in the process of learning how to sell Proteus services. She has been a coach and facilitator for many years, and has mostly focused on delivering those services rather than selling them herself. Now she wants to build her own client relationships. She's raised her level of aspiration around learning the skill of consultative selling, and feels ready to do it. As she's getting more self-aware and more curious, though, she's realizing that the "skill" of selling actually consists of a whole group

of subskills, some of which she's great at (listening, for instance, and diagnosing someone's real needs), and some of which are pretty new to her (making quick matches between need and offer, and moving to agreement).

As I reflected on her question, I realized that it's only necessary to focus on "sub-aspiration" if you run into a roadblock inside yourself as you're learning the whole set of skills. In other words, your overall aspiration to learn a complex skill set may carry you through all the necessary sub-learning. If so, that's great. But if you've been learning a complex skill set and suddenly find yourself drifting away from making the needed effort...look to see if you've run into not wanting to learn some subskill that's a critical part of the overall learning.

I've been seeing this happen with another colleague of mine who's also decided she wants to build her own client base. For a while she was making a pretty consistent effort to learn, and was starting to generate some interest among likely prospects. Then, over a period of time, I noticed that her effort fell off. She was making all the normal excuses about why that was happening (too busy, got distracted, other priorities, etc.). But when we talked through it, she saw that she was stuck on a particular subskill. She didn't feel comfortable shifting conversations with potential clients from social chat to "let's talk about whether we might do business together." When she recognized that this was a critical subskill she needed in order to sell, she realized she had to shift herself into wanting to learn that subskill.

One good thing about aspiration is that it's quite easy to tell whether or not you have it. If you're not actually taking steps to do something, then you don't really want to do it, no matter what you're telling yourself. Your aspiration is insufficient. Period.

It's a great immediate simple feedback loop. Not making effort to learn? Not enough aspiration. Making effort to learn? Aspiration is in place. Once you've accepted this, you'll be much better able to work on increasing your aspiration, rather than falling prey to all the other reasons your mind presents to explain why you're not doing something.

Neutral Self-Awareness

Q: I think I'm better than others give me credit for. Maybe they're just not seeing what I'm capable of.

You may be right—it could be that people aren't seeing you clearly. However, it's more likely that there's another issue at play here. You may be confusing your current capability with your potential. In other words, people are assessing you based on what they see you doing right now, and you're assessing yourself based on what you believe you're capable of doing. This is a really common stumbling block to becoming neutrally self-aware.

Recently, I was talking to a new manager about her employee. He's the first person she's ever managed, and they're having this problem: she sees what he's doing, and he's focusing on what he thinks he's capable of doing. This guy isn't performing very well at his current job, and he keeps asking her for a promotion. When she says, "I don't feel you're ready for a promotion," he says, "Oh, I'm definitely ready. I could do a much bigger job."

She's assessing him neutrally, in a fair witness way, and coming to a logical conclusion: "I don't observe you doing the job you have to a high standard; I have no reason to believe you could do a bigger, more demanding job to a high standard." He's not referencing the facts of the situation at all: he's basing his self-assessment on what he believes would be possible for him. That's not neutral self-awareness, that's unwarranted hopefulness.

If you find that you consistently think you're better at things than other people think you are, you may be caught in this confusion. Here's a way to resolve it: it's fairly simple, but it requires a certain degree of bravery on your part, and the discipline of being a fair witness about yourself.

First, of those people who think a particular skill isn't a strength of yours (when you do), pick the one in whom you have the most trust. That is, choose the person you believe is most often fair and accurate, even though you may not see eye to eye in this instance. Ask the person to describe to you, as specifically as possible, the difference between how she sees you performing right now in this area and what she would consider "good."

As the person speaks, really focus your attention on getting curious and trying to fully understand what she is seeing (this will help keep your self-talk from drifting into defending yourself, making excuses, or figuring out why the person is wrong). Your goal in this conversation is to understand and write down a few things the person says that seem accurate to you and that define the gap between what you're doing now and "good"—that is, two or three behaviors that someone who was "good" at this skill would do that you are not now doing.

If you're able to do this exercise, it will help you begin to make that very important distinction between "what I can do now" and "what I might be capable of, once I learn more." Being able to accurately make this distinction is key to neutral self-awareness, and is an essential element of being a high-payoff learner.

Even though this exercise is simple, you may find it very difficult, even scary. If you find yourself having a really hard time understanding what the person is saying, or if you can't help interrupting to disagree, or if you find yourself getting angry, I suspect that you're stumbling over something inside yourself that we've talked about quite a bit: you may believe that you're not capable of getting better at this skill. If so, no wonder it's difficult for you to accept that you're not good at it right now—that would mean (in your mind) that you're doomed *never* to be good at it.

In that case, you need to unearth and shift that self-talk. If you realize that voice in your head is saying some version of, *You'll never get any better at this*, remind yourself of a few things you've gotten better at in the past few years (even something simple, like getting familiar with a social media site, cooking a new dish, or learning to play an online game), and tell yourself, *I've gotten better at lots of things; I can get better at this. It's okay to acknowledge that I'm not good at it yet.*

Q: How can I have an accurate sense of how good I am at something I don't know anything about yet?
This is a great question, and it's why having good "sources" is so important. You may remember that when we were talking about finding sources for feedback, in chapter 5, I noted three important qualities of good sources: they see you clearly, want the best for you, and are willing to be honest with you.

There's one additional quality to look for when you're asking a source to assess you in an area where you're a true novice. That person needs to have some expertise in that area. That way, he will be able to compare your current level of skill to his understanding of what "good" looks like in the area where you're trying to learn, and he can tell you how big the gap is (similar to what we talked about in the question above).

In addition, if the skill you're trying to learn is either physical or knowledge based, your sources might also be able to direct you to some objective skill testing to find out your initial level of ability. We all spent our school years taking these kinds of tests: testing how fast you could run a quarter mile or whether you could name the capitals of all the countries in South America.

Unfortunately, it's much more difficult to find those kinds of tests for many of the complex skills we need to acquire these days—skills requiring a combination of knowledge, interactive skills, value judgment, and information patterning, like selling, managing people, or developing products, to name just a few. In order to discover your starting point in that kind of skill, a good source is most often your best bet. Find someone who is good at the skill and has those three key "source" qualities, and ask her for an honest assessment of your current capability. And then—this is critical—listen to what that person has to say with your best fair witness mindset.

Q: Okay, I'm embarrassed. I've just gotten some feedback, and it looks like I'm not as good at something as I thought I was. What do I do now?

That *is* embarrassing. Especially if it's all happening in a relatively public setting, like work. The executives we coach sometimes find themselves in this situation at the start of their coaching engagement. They've been going along in their career, thinking they're doing great (because no one ever said otherwise), and then suddenly, their boss lets them know they're going to have to learn some new skills, or do some things differently or better, in order to keep succeeding. I've had many executives begin our first phone call by explaining (with more than a tinge of self-justification) why they're being offered a coach.

This is a place where the need for neutral self-awareness combines with the need to be willing to "be bad first"—and, as you now know, shifting your self-talk is key to both.

When we find out that we're not doing as well as we thought in some area that's important to us (managing or leading others, for instance, or staying up to date in our core area of expertise), our first impulse is often to try to invalidate the feedback, so we don't have to accept the embarrassing reality of being less good than we thought we were. Here's how that sounds inside our heads, as self-talk: *That's ridiculous—what do my employees know anyway?* or *Well, I just haven't been at my best these past few months* or *All those people giving the feedback are jealous of me* or . . . you get the picture. Some people stay in that mode indefinitely: we all know people who have the perfect excuse for every piece of critical feedback they've ever gotten. If you don't want to be one of those people, make it your business to listen to feedback about yourself with an open, fair witness, curious mindset.

So, let's say you've moved past defensiveness or blame, and are realizing that the feedback has some basis in truth. What often happens at that point is that our self-talk shifts into beating us up unmercifully: *I'm such an idiot—why didn't I know/do/see that before?* And then that interior monologue often goes on to predict catastrophic failure as a result of our self-assessed "idiocy": *My boss will probably fire me* or *Now nobody will trust me* or *I might as well quit—everybody will be laughing at me anyway.*

With self-talk like this, who needs enemies? When the voice in your head is making dire predictions, it's no wonder you're feeling awful!

Here's a suggestion for shifting your self-talk so that it will serve you better. Once you realize you're less good at something than you thought you were, you can say to yourself: *It's definitely awkward finding out that I'm not as good as I thought I was. But now I know (or can find out) what to do about it. And if I let people know that I'm working on getting better, it's likely they'll be supportive of my willingness to improve rather than judgmental about my need to improve.* If this particular self-talk isn't believable to you, craft a version for yourself that is. The main goal of whatever self-talk you create at this juncture, though, is to accept any negative feelings you're having in response to the feedback (embarrassment, frustration, dejection) and then help yourself move through them, to get to hopefulness and a focus on learning.

Q: I grade myself really hard—it's difficult to acknowledge my strengths. How can I change that?
I recently spent a week doing brief individual coaching sessions with a group of high-potential mid-level managers. During their

sessions, a great many of them shared with me their realization that they are much harder on themselves than anyone else is—that they consistently judge themselves harshly and underestimate their skills and potential. One woman in particular—who, by any objective measure, was intelligent, focused, and successful in her career—was burdened with especially nasty self-talk. That voice in her head was consistent in pointing out her (mostly imagined) mistakes, telling her she was bound to fail, and insisting that others were smarter, more articulate, and just all-around better than she was.

I encouraged her to become more of a fair witness of herself, but she was really stuck. For every objective fact the "fair witness voice" of her self-talk pointed out (*You've been promoted three times in the past four years*) the "unfair critic voice" had an immediate comeback (*And now they probably regret promoting you*). Finally, I asked, "Do you have anyone else in your life who undermines you like this and only says negative, hurtful things about you?"

She looked taken aback. "Of course not. My family and friends are very supportive, especially my husband."

"Okay," I said. "What would you do if you did have a friend who behaved like that toward you?"

"I think I'd avoid that person. Why would I want to spend time with somebody who was mean to me all the time?"

"Exactly," I said. I just looked at her for a few moments, till I saw understanding dawn in her eyes. "Why are you so willing to be mean to yourself?" I added.

We don't have to put up with our own unfair, ungenerous, unkind assessments of ourselves. We can disagree with that "critic" voice. We can "talk back" to that negative voice and stand up for ourselves in the same way a good friend or loving family member would do. We can shift our self-talk about ourselves to be fair, kind, and generous; we can support our own success.

Endless Curiosity

Q: But some things are just BORING. How can I possibly get curious about stuff that makes me want to go to sleep?

I beg to differ. I'm not sure anything is intrinsically boring. The *Merriam-Webster Dictionary* defines boredom as "the state of being weary and restless through lack of interest." You notice that definition doesn't ascribe boredom to the thing about which one is bored; it says that boredom arises from lack of interest.

I had a friend for many years who found lots of things boring. When people would start to talk about them, he'd lose focus and his attention would drift or he'd start to interrupt, to change the subject to something that was more to his liking. He was very interested— sometimes almost obsessively so—in certain things. But because he believed that most things were boring, his life was quite circumscribed. I noticed that he had a hard time enjoying travel, for instance, and that his career didn't really progress: he stayed focused in the one area he found interesting. Once I even heard him tell one of his kids, when she was chattering about her friends at school, "Why would I be interested in hearing about that?"

In order to engage your endless curiosity, you have to first stop listening to the voice in your head that's insisting, *Some things are just BORING.* See if, instead, you can get curious about what might be interesting about a thing you're assuming is boring. Let's say, for instance, that your boss is telling you about a new process that's being put in place for tracking inventory of your key products. *So boring*, you think to yourself. And yet you realize that you need to have at least enough interest in it to learn to use it. So, you might want to ask yourself, *Why is my boss so excited about this?* or *How might this make my job easier?* or even, *I wonder if this is really better than the previous process, or if it's just somebody's goofy idea?* (Even skepticism will bring you closer to curiosity than disinterest will.)

Pretty much any *Why, How,* or *I wonder* question will do...you're just looking for one thing in this so-called boring topic about which you can be interested.

Don't get me wrong—I'm not saying that the inventory tracking process will ever become your favorite thing, or even something you find more than mildly interesting. My point is that it is possible to get interested in anything. And that's a much more useful belief to hold than the belief that some things are by their very nature uninteresting, and can't ever be anything but boring. Holding *that* belief will limit you from a lot of learning.

Q: Can you be too curious?

If you define curiosity as "a deep need to understand and master," then I doubt it's possible to be too curious.

However, there are some things that masquerade as curiosity and thereby give it a bad name. For instance, I know of some people who simply want to be in control of everything around them, and they excuse it by naming their intrusive questioning "curiosity." For example, the manager who sends thirty e-mails asking whether something has been done, and then giving direction about how to do it masked as curious questions (e.g., "I wonder if you've thought about calling the head of research and asking him to allocate half of one person's time to the project for the next few weeks?"). If confronted, that manager might say, "I was just curious about how the project was going." Remember, curiosity is "wanting to understand something and get better at doing it." Micromanaging, even if it's disguised as curiosity, is "thinking you already understand something and that you need to make other people better at doing it."

Another kind of fake curiosity is what I call "endless divergent thinking." A client of mine was complaining to me recently about her boss, the CEO of the company, telling me that he was "too curious." When I asked her what she meant, she replied that he was fond of having extended brainstorming sessions, where he asked the team to come up with lots of ideas for improving the business. But then he never asked them to select which ones to pursue, or to figure out what they would have to do to make them happen. Again, if you go back to our definition of curiosity as a deep need to understand and master, this isn't that. Brainstorming can be a good first step in being curious—a good brainstorm can surface some great possibilities—but if you don't follow it up by taking a few of those ideas deeper and using them to improve the business, that's not real curiosity. It's a waste of mental and emotional energy that could be better put to use for real learning.

I see the appeal, though—if you just focus on generating cool ideas, you never have to do the hard work of being bad first as you're trying to bring those ideas to fruition. Real curiosity, of which I believe we can never have too much, leads you seamlessly into being bad first. Fake curiosity avoids it.

Q: I'm worried I'll look dumb if I ask questions that demonstrate my lack of knowledge or understanding. What if I'm the only one who doesn't know?

I don't believe I have ever had anyone think I'm dumb for asking a curious question, or revealing my lack of knowledge. And people pay me a good deal of money to advise and teach them, so it's fair to assume they're expecting a pretty high degree of knowledge and expertise from me. In fact, there are two things I say almost every day, both of which reveal my lack of understanding. The first is, "I'm not sure I understand what you're saying—could you say more or explain it differently?" And the second is, "How is what you're talking about different from (or similar to) this other thing?"

I'm convinced that the problem with asking curious questions is not that we actually look dumb, it's that we *think* we'll look dumb, and that makes us pose the question in an I'm-afraid-you'll-think-I'm-dumb-for-asking-this-question way. For example, when we think we're going to look dumb for asking a question, we speak softly, look down, bite our lip, or hem and haw. We might even apologize for asking it, or—worst of all—preface our question by saying something like, "I know you'll think I'm an idiot for not knowing this, but..." Yikes.

So that takes us, as usual, back to our self-talk. If you believe, and are therefore thinking to yourself, *If I ask this question, everyone will think I'm dumb,* you'll almost certainly pose your question in a way that reveals that belief—and makes it a self-fulfilling prophecy.

One way to shift your self-talk in this area is to think of someone you respect who's willing to ask "novice" questions. Ask yourself, *Do I think that person looks dumb when he asks an I-don't-know type question?* I suspect that your answer will be no—and that, in fact, you may realize that you have respect for people who are willing to do that. My dad, a very smart guy and an excellent lawyer, was also extremely curious, and would often say to people, "Wow, I don't know much about that—how does that work?" I was always impressed that he had the self-confidence to reveal his lack of knowledge like that, without worrying what people would think. I got the impression that finding out something new was more important to him than whether other people judged him for not knowing.

One caveat, however: there is a kind of question—even if it's curiosity based—that *does* look dumb. If someone has taken the time to explain something to you, or to share with you material that explains it (and you've committed to reviewing the material), and then you ask an I-don't-know question about something simple that's covered in that material...then people may very well think you're not so bright. They may also think that you're either lazy or disrespectful. Many years ago, we had someone working for us who used to do this: we'd go over a topic on a phone call, and then she'd ask a question about it that had just been answered. And I'm not talking about questions that would take her knowledge deeper; this person would ask for specific information that had just been shared. (For instance, on one call, someone said, "We'll need to have everything ready for the client by the end of next week," and a few minutes later this person asked, "When do we need to have the materials ready for the client?")

So, don't hesitate to ask curious questions about things that are new to you: almost everyone who hears you will see you as being self-confident and self-motivated, and you'll be turbocharging your learning.

Q: When people talk about things I don't know about, I lose focus fast. How can I stay engaged?
When someone is discussing a topic that's new to you, there are two basic directions your mind can take. The first is disinterest—usually accompanied by self-talk like, *I don't know or care about this—I'll just think about something else till they're done talking.* The second is curiosity—and as we now know, the self-talk of curiosity shows up mostly as *How . . . Why . . .* or *I wonder . . .* questions.

If you're losing focus, it means you're walking down the path of disinterested self-talk. The best way to re-engage yourself is to ask a curiosity-based question about the topic, and then listen to the answer. It's best to ask it aloud—that will both demonstrate your interest to the speaker and keep you more focused (we tend to want to hear the answers to questions we've asked). But even if you can only ask the question to yourself mentally (if you're at a lecture, for instance, or listening to a recording of someone speaking), it will still help to move you from disinterest and disengagement to interest and engagement.

If, for whatever reason, you find yourself unable to come up with a curiosity-based question, there's another thing you can try. Set yourself the goal of summarizing, either aloud or as a written note to yourself, the essence of what the other person is saying. For example, let's say a colleague is reviewing a big project she has been working on—something far outside your area of expertise—and you find your attention drifting. If you can't think of a curious question, set yourself the task of summarizing and writing down the essence of what she is communicating in a couple of sentences. I'll bet that you'll find yourself much more focused on what she is saying.

Here's why this works: in order to be able to summarize something someone is saying, you have to understand it. If you're trying to understand what someone is saying well enough to summarize it, you begin listening *as though you were curious*—because the essence of curiosity is the need to understand. And once you're paying attention to something in this trying-to-understand way, your actual curiosity often gets catalyzed, and you find yourself engaged in the topic. Try it and see...

Willingness to Be Bad First

Q: Come on. You're telling me it's okay to be bad at my job?
I'm telling you it's okay to be bad at those parts of your job that you haven't yet had the opportunity to learn. For example, let's say that you were a UX (user experience) manager at web development Company A, and then you get a job as a senior UX manager at web development Company B. If I'm your new boss at Company B, I'm going to expect you to be good at understanding what creates good UX, and at being able to manage UX folks to determine how to improve the user experience within a website or other project. That's why I hired you, and I'm going to be deeply unhappy if you don't have the expertise I expect in those areas.

However, I'm not going to expect you to know all about Company B at the beginning—how we do things, what our philosophy is, or who the important people are and how they work. In fact, I'd be suspicious if you pretended you were already "good" at that, and didn't ask a whole bunch of curiosity-based questions in your first few months. I'm also, if I'm a reasonably good manager, going to recognize that this is a bigger, more senior job than you had at

Company A—that for the first time you're managing managers, and that you'll have things to learn about doing that well. I'm also going to realize that your area of expertise—just like everything else in web design—is changing daily, and that you're going to be running into new things that you (and all your folks) will be "bad" at until you learn them. In fact, if I don't see you as being willing to be "bad at" the new developments in your field on a pretty regular basis, I'm going to start to worry as your manager, because it will mean that your team, and Company B, are going to get left behind.

Q: The idea of "being bad" at something in front of people (especially the people I work for and the ones who work for me) makes me very nervous. What can I do to make it easier?

Just as in every other area of learning, practice makes perfect: the more you practice "being bad" in public, the easier it gets. The first time you're running a meeting and someone who works for you says something you don't understand, and you take a deep breath and say, "I'm not sure I'm following you—could you explain that in a different way?" it's going to feel awkward and even a little scary. But then the person will stop and say, "Oh, sure. This was something we found out from the salespeople. We asked them about last year's..." You'll listen and understand; the other person will feel important and helpful; and the trust and openness on your team will tick up a few micro-points. In other words, nothing bad will happen—and, in fact, a number of good things will happen. That will make it much easier to "be bad" the next time, and the next. Word will get around that you're really interested in your folks and good to work for, better conversations will happen, and your employees will start to ask curious questions of their own in meetings. You and your team will be experiencing much more high-payoff learning than before.

And before you try this for the first time, as you're revising your self-talk to support you in being bad first, feel free to use any or all of the preceding paragraph as fodder for your learning-supportive self-talk!

Q: Isn't this just about "failing fast"?

No, although there is a connection. "Failing fast" or "failing forward" have become very popular concepts over the past decade or so; what people generally mean when they use one of those phrases is that in order to break new ground in any area, we have to be willing to fail numerous times, and then to bounce back quickly from failure and keep going. I completely agree with this premise—and I think the fact that this idea has become so popular is yet another symptom of the speed at which everything around us is changing. Unlike past eras, when only a few people at the edges of science and industry had to worry about breaking new ground, in this era almost all of us are breaking new ground, in ways large and small, on a daily basis.

Recognizing that you will experience failure when learning new things, and accepting that, is indeed part of being willing to be bad first. And the balancing self-talk of accepting not-good plus self-belief will definitely help you continue through failure.

However, the ANEW model offers other essential tools—the things you need for mastering much more than just the "failure" part of learning. You now know how to ramp up your *aspiration*, so you can actually focus on learning those things you need to learn. You know how to get clearer about your own current capabilities and mindset—to improve your *neutral self-awareness*—so that you have a more accurate understanding of where you're starting from in your learning. You also know how to rediscover and engage your own *endless curiosity*, so you can harness the wonderful power of your brain and will to understand and master new topics. And finally, you have the tools to build the mental skill of *willingness to be bad first*, which will support you not only through actual failures, but through the even more common slowness, awkwardness, and disorientation that accompany all new learning.

In fact, we've found that using the ANEW skills makes it less likely that you'll experience major failure on the road to new learning. It turns out that a fairly high proportion of big failures arise from either lack of neutral self-awareness or lack of curiosity. For example, a few years ago, a respected nonprofit company where a friend of mine was working decided that it wanted to engage more of its patrons in taking advantage of the educational classes offered by the organization. The classes would provide an additional source of funds, the organization's leaders reasoned, as well as carrying the nonprofit's educational mission to a larger group of people. My friend, who was the head of the IT department, cautioned that the software platform they were considering using for class scheduling was not best suited for their needs, and also that the licensing fees were so expensive that it would be difficult to make a profit unless class participation increased enormously. The organization's executive director wasn't interested in hearing about the potential problems with the platform and refused to acknowledge that the organization might not have the skills needed to market the classes well enough to create the needed participation. He was neither curious nor neutrally self-aware.

Sadly, the effort was an embarrassing and expensive failure—and the executive director characterized it to his board as an example of "failing forward"—asserting that failures like this are an inevitable part of being innovative and assuring them that he and the organization had learned from this mistake and would be able to "do it right" the next time. I suspect, though, that without some work on the "N" and "E" skills of ANEW, this nonprofit may be in for yet more failures in this realm.

My experience and observation lead me to believe that employing all four of the ANEW skills is the most efficient and fastest way to learn new things—reducing failures, speeding up the cycle time from novice to expert, and positioning you well for your next round of new learning in the same area.

Q: Shouldn't we play to our strengths? Why should I try to do things that I'm bad at?
We should definitely play to our strengths. That's why neutral self-awareness is such an essential part of real learning. If I can't carry a tune in a bucket, I should be clear about that, so I don't stake my future happiness on my ability to become a world-class singer, as per our *American Idol* example in chapter 5. But there's a big difference between being bad at something because you have no capacity to improve and being bad at something because you haven't learned to do it yet. And I suspect that "playing to our strengths" in the sense of "only doing those things that you're good at right now" is not really going to be an option for any of us in the months and years to come.

The good news is that the sweet spot of learning is being able to play to your strengths *in order* to get good at things that you're now bad at doing. For example, let's say that you know one of your key strengths is that you're kind of relentless. That is, if you decide to do something, you'll just keep chipping away at it till it's done. That's a key strength you can leverage in order to keep going through the "being bad" part of any new learning. Or perhaps you're really good at seeing patterns and similarities between things, at understanding the underlying principles that make one thing like another. That's going to be tremendously helpful when it comes to "bridging" from what you already know and can do, to what you're just learning. Or you may be wonderful at building relationships. That will serve you well when you're looking for sources to help increase your neutral self-awareness, and when you need to find people you can ask curious questions about the things you're learning.

In other words, rather than using your strengths as a limitation on your future learning, use them as a lever for learning even more and better.

Q: Do you ever get done being bad?

My husband asked this wonderful question. And my answer was, not if you're lucky. If you never get done being bad, it means you're still learning, creating new understanding and capability for yourself.

Even in the areas where we're most experienced and the most expert, we can always keep trying new things, going back to being bad in order to get better. A great recent example for me was writing this book. Before I started writing *Be Bad First*, I had published three business books, finished a big historical novel (still sitting on my computer), and written hundreds of proposals, blog posts, workbooks, and marketing pieces. I consider myself a good and fluent writer, and have gotten a lot of external feedback in support of that perception. As I thought about writing this book, I decided to try some new things. I wanted this book to be more research based and faster paced, different in a number of ways from my previous books. I wrote the first third of it, trying my new approach, and shared it with Jim Levine, my agent. He gave me some very honest feedback, the essence of which was, "This has potential, but it's not great, and here are the reasons why." I used my willing-to-be-bad-first self-talk (*I'm trying something new, so I'm bad at it to begin with, and I can get better*) and did some more bridging from what had worked in my previous books. I rewrote the part Jim had commented on; it felt much better. I got on a roll of combining the new elements with the style of my previous books, and was able to create the book you're reading now.

In fact, I've noticed that those people who are most truly masters of mastery feel as though they're always learning, always finding areas where they're "bad" (even if only relative to their own existing expertise) and can get better. Pablo Casals, perhaps the greatest classical cellist of the twentieth century, was asked, at the age of ninety-three, why he continued to practice his cello three hours a day. He replied, "I'm beginning to notice some improvement..."

Pile o' Topics

Stuck self-talk: I've tried to change my self-talk, but it's like a rubber band—it just keeps going back to the old shape. Can I actually change it?

I once coached an executive, a woman whose parents had been very critical of her when she was growing up and had consistently discounted her intelligence. Even at the point she and I worked together, when she was in her late forties and they in their seventies, their negative, demeaning voices were still with her daily—in the form of her self-talk. Especially in challenging situations, she would find herself thinking, *You're just not smart enough to figure this out* and *Everyone will find out you're not capable of doing this job.* Even though she knew rationally that these messages weren't accurate, she couldn't seem to shake them. Even when she created realistic, hopeful alternative self-talk, like, *I've demonstrated my intelligence and capability many times; I know I can do my job well,* she would find herself reverting again and again to her old, unsupportive self-talk. It was exhausting and frustrating for her—and it was making it very difficult for her to become curious or to be willing to be bad first; both felt too risky, given the way she was talking to herself.

After some trial and error, we finally landed on an approach that worked for her. First, whenever, she talked about her parents, or about her lack of faith in herself, I noticed that her posture changed: she scrunched her shoulders forward, tucked her chin a little, and often crossed her arms, assuming an almost protective posture. Her voice also got thinner and softer, which led me to believe that her breathing was constrained.

The next time I saw it happening, I encouraged her to stop talking and focus on her body for a moment. I asked her to relax her shoulders, raise her head a bit, and uncross her arms; then I suggested she take three deep breaths, relaxing her stomach and gently pulling the air all the way down to her diaphragm.

I asked her how she felt. "Good," she said, sounding surprised, her voice stronger.

"Now try thinking your revised self-talk, and see how it hits you," I suggested.

She paused for a few moments. I noticed that her chin was up and her shoulders were down—she *looked* more confident and relaxed.

"It seems more true now," she said at last, still sounding somewhat surprised. "I believe it. I am doing my job well—and have been doing it well consistently."

It wasn't magic: she didn't suddenly become free of all of her unhelpful self-talk. But she *was* significantly less "stuck"; after that point, when her mind was really kicking her ass, she could generally remember to relax and straighten her body and deepen her breathing, and it made a big difference in her ability to shift her self-talk in a more accurate and hopeful direction.

As it turns out, I wasn't just making this up. A good deal of research has shown that there is a strong connection between what we do with our bodies and how we feel. For example, in 1989 two psychologists named Pamela Adelmann and Robert Zajonc published a detailed study on the emotional effects of smiling.[1] Using a variety of approaches and subjects, they found a strong correlation between producing a physical smile and feeling happy, even when the smile was produced by, for instance, making a long "e" sound . . . an emotion-neutral approach that logically should have had no impact on the subject's level of happiness.

Often, when we find ourselves caught in cycles of self-critical belief, we unconsciously breathe and hold our bodies in ways that reflect fear, uncertainty, self-protection: tensing our shoulders, breathing shallowly, lowering our eyes, clasping our hands. If we consciously shift into relaxing and opening up our body and our breathing—which is what happens when we feel confident and open—we're more likely to be able to "hear" and believe the more confident and open self-talk we've devised.

Fear: When I think about learning some things I know I need to learn—like public speaking—it's terrifying. What can I do about that?

Fear is powerful. In the best cases, it can be a lifesaving reaction to true threat: we're all fortunate to have been born with this response built into us. The problem is, even though we are not now being pursued by large predators or attacked by rival clansmen on a daily basis, we still often react as though we were.

In this modern age, our fear can become chronic, a daily impediment to living the lives we want to live and are capable of living. And our day-to-day fears are often directed at things that pose no actual danger to us: regarding this particular question, research shows that about 75 percent of people have a profound fear of speaking in public. For many, it is their deepest fear. What, exactly, are we afraid of here? Speaking in public won't kill us; it won't even hurt us. At worst, we might look foolish or incompetent. And yet, millions of people say they're *more afraid of speaking in public than they are of dying.* (Jerry Seinfeld famously joked about this statistic by noting that the average person at a funeral would rather be in the coffin than delivering the eulogy.)

At least with public speaking, folks generally know they're afraid. The most insidious fears are those we're not consciously aware of—because they can impede our learning and growth without our knowledge. For example, a number of years ago I coached an executive who was deeply unhappy in her job. Her boss, the CEO, was a really bad guy (arrogant, shortsighted, mean-spirited, and not very smart), and she had much less autonomy and influence than she deserved, given her skills and experience. I worked with her to create an exit strategy, and she developed a clear and feasible plan for herself, complete with actions and timelines. There was a big component of new learning involved, because she had been at her company for many years, and had never really looked for a job. She seemed to be focusing well on all the ANEW skills in making her plan, and it sounded to me as though her aspiration, neutral self-awareness, curiosity, and willingness to be bad first were all in pretty good shape. Yet when I met with her to check on her progress, she hadn't done any of the things she'd committed to only a month before.

I asked her why, and she offered a flurry of excuses—too busy, couldn't get hold of the people on her list, no jobs in her field, dog ate my homework, etc., etc. I asked her what she could have done differently to overcome those obstacles, and she said, in effect, that they were all totally out of her control. I sat back, puzzled. Then I decided to just reflect back to her what I was seeing and hearing.

"So," I said, "You're completely stuck. You really have no way of leaving your current job." She stared at me for a moment, speechless—and then burst into tears.

After composing herself, she said she had just realized that she wasn't making effort to move forward with her plan because she was, quite simply, afraid.

We then had a very honest conversation about what was scary for her: she hadn't looked for a job in more than a decade and worried about interviewing badly; her boss's constant criticism had made her question her competence; she was concerned her husband might not support her decision. This was a whole new level of neutral self-awareness for her—not only getting clear about where she was starting from, but also how she felt about it. When we had surfaced those specific fears, we talked about how she could move through them. It was slow going, but once she recognized her fears, she was able to address them. At that point, she was free to work her plan and learn the skills she needed to learn. About eight months later she found a new job, reporting to someone she liked and respected, and doing challenging work for which she is both appreciated and compensated.

If you want to free yourself from the limiting effects of fear, try this:

Acknowledge it. My client's breakthrough came when she realized that her reasons were just excuses. Take a look at something you say you want to learn and aren't learning, especially if you've identified benefits of learning it that are meaningful to you, and envisioned a future where you have those benefits, but still aren't making the effort to learn. Listen to how your internal monologue justifies not doing it. Now imagine that you're a neutral third party listening to your self-talk. What would that person think you're afraid of in this situation? You may be surprised how clear it is to you what you fear, once you're looking through the eyes of your fictional fair witness. As soon as you can say to yourself, *I'm afraid that* _____, you're halfway to being free of that fear.

Ask: What's the worst? Once you've spoken your fear, ask yourself, *What's the very worst thing that could happen if I do this?* Really let yourself go all the way down the path, to the worst possible outcome. For instance, *If I leave this job, I might never get another. I could become homeless, go crazy, and die of starvation and exposure.* Then ask, *How likely is this to happen?* Be as objective as possible in your answer. I suspect an objective answer would be some version of, *It's extremely unlikely.* Just getting to this point in the process will quite often make you feel much less afraid and resistant; it's like turning on the light when you're a kid, afraid in the dark: *Oh look, that monster is just my shirt hung over the chair.*

Address it. Ask, *What can I do to make it even less likely that the worst will happen?* This is where your brain starts to engage in practical problem-solving (which in itself is a wonderful antidote to fear).

In the example above, you might decide not to leave your job till you have another one lined up or you may decide not to leave till you have six months of living expenses saved and a part-time job arranged to fall back on if you need it. Articulate what will make you feel as though you're reducing "the worst" to a vanishingly small possibility.

Act. Finally, take one small step in the direction that you fear: anything will do. Update your résumé. Create a better online profile. Have lunch with someone whose company is hiring. Ask a friend a curious question about how she found a new job. Doing a simple action that pushes up against your fear, and finding that nothing bad happens as a result, can be liberating out of all proportion to the import of the act itself. You'll find the next step is much easier, and the next.

And once you've acknowledged, addressed, and are beginning to act in defiance of your fear, you'll be much better able to apply your ANEW skills. Without the mental, emotional, and physical static of fear to confuse and impede you, you'll be on your own path to mastery.

Dilettantism: I like this book, and it makes sense. I would like to get better at learning… but I often feel that way when I read a new "how-to" book. Then I drift. Is there something I can do to increase my chances of sticking with learning ANEW—or anything?
First, I'd remind you of the difference between thinking something might be cool to do (that is, being mildly interested in it) and truly wanting to do it. Unless you actually aspire to learn something, as we've defined it here, it's unlikely that you'll do it. I, like you, have read lots of how-to books, and thought, *Yeah, that would be good*… but haven't had enough real aspiration to carry me forward. So, if you'd truly like to take advantage of what you've read here, you'll need to identify the personal benefits to you of building your

ANEW skills, and then envision a future where you'll be reaping those benefits.

And if you do decide that you actually (versus theoretically) want to get better at ANEW, you then need to do something practical to make that happen—and pretty quickly. We've found, in our coaching and training work, that people are most successful at incorporating new skills into their lives if they have rewarding experiences using them right away. That's one reason there are so many activities throughout this book—I wanted to give you a real taste of the benefits of applying these skills. And that's the whole reason for the next and final chapter—it's a complete walk-through, in which you practice applying all the skills. I'll be guiding you through it step by step, so you can start building an immediate momentum of success with ANEW. If you want to learn these skills, I'm here to help: I definitely want you to learn them and to derive all the benefits of using them.

So, if you'd like some more support for making these skills a part of your toolkit—here you go . . .

CHAPTER 9

Do It Now: Making ANEW
Your Own

I am still learning.

—Michelangelo

This great one-liner was supposedly Michelangelo's standard response when someone complimented his work. When I first heard this, it explained a lot to me about Michelangelo's astonishing accomplishments: I realized that he saw learning as an endless and exciting path, full of new possibilities and opportunities for mastery. He was a true master of ANEW. And he did keep learning; Michelangelo lived to be eighty-eight years old—in an era when living into one's sixties was considered a long life—and kept exploring new things until the day he died. For instance, in 1546, when he was seventy-one, he took on another commission from the Vatican, this one for two enormous frescos telling the stories of the conversion of Saint Paul and the crucifixion of Saint Peter. In these frescoes, he experimented with perspective in a way that was misunderstood for centuries. Both paintings seem out of proportion when viewed frontally, and many people thought that this was an indication of Michelangelo's failing eyesight or that he was somehow losing his craft. However, later scholars realized that he had constructed the paintings so that they would look accurate when viewed from below, as they would be, since they were painted high on the walls of the chapel in the Vatican Palace.

As if that wasn't enough to take on in his seventy-first year, he was also appointed in that same year to be the architect for St. Peter's Basilica. The structure had been under construction for almost forty years, and a series of architects had made little progress. As he was completing the frescos, he redesigned the plans for the basilica, building on what had been done before but designing changes to make the existing structure both stronger and more beautiful. He worked on the basilica until his death in 1564; it was completed many years later, largely to his specifications. It is one of the two largest churches in the world, and generally agreed to be the most well-known work of Renaissance architecture.

We may not be Michelangelo, but we can each unleash our full power to learn, to master new skills and capabilities. Becoming a high-payoff learner is our key to succeeding in this time of change . . . and will allow us to continue to thrive as change accelerates.

Let's get to it. I've offered you activities throughout the book to give you a chance to try each skill as we've discussed it. In this final chapter, we'll go through the entire process of applying all four ANEW skills in some area that's really important for you to learn. Think of this chapter as an individual coaching session with me: insofar as possible, I'll guide you through this process as I would if we were sitting in a room together. (For even more of that coaching experience, I invite you to visit bebadfirst.com and watch a video version of this chapter. And you'll find a framework for note taking in the writeable PDF you downloaded earlier.)

Let's Get Started . . .

Our first order of business is for you to pick a topic. What's something that you feel you really need to learn? You can pick something you already want to learn, which will make the *aspiration* part easier, or you can pick something you don't want to learn (even though you need to), if you want to raise the degree of difficulty and give yourself a chance to try building your aspiration.

As a thought starter, here are a few of the skills I've noticed people (myself included) learning recently:

➤ Giving feedback
➤ Creating e-learning courses
➤ Gluten-free cooking
➤ Delegation
➤ Managing a P&L
➤ Presentation skills
➤ Building websites
➤ Increasing executive presence
➤ Yoga
➤ Running a nonprofit
➤ Using Salesforce
➤ Podcasting
➤ Gardening
➤ Thinking and acting strategically
➤ Knitting
➤ Listening
➤ Craft brewing
➤ Leading change
➤ Swing dancing

You'll notice that the preceding list includes a mix of "work" and "personal" topics—we've found that learning is learning, and that ANEW works in any area.

Pick a skill or capability—from this list or not—that's important to you, one that you personally believe you must have in order to create the life you want.

> The skill or capability you'll focus on learning in this chapter:

Building Aspiration

Now let's think about the benefits you'll derive from learning this skill. Remember, in order to generate real aspiration, these benefits must be personally meaningful to you. If you already want to learn this topic, this part will be easy—you will already have thought of those meaningful benefits. You can just note them.

If you've decided to go for the tougher option, though, and have picked a topic that you need to learn but don't want to, this step is critical. As you start to think about the possible benefits to you of learning this skill, you can use the approach we discussed earlier, of focusing on benefits you already know are important to you, and seeing if they apply to this topic. For example (just to pick one from the list above), let's say you've decided that it's important for you to become a better listener, but you aren't really motivated to learn to do that. When you think about some skills you've learned recently, perhaps you remember how motivating it is for you to have more and better tools for developing and responding to your employees. You realize that you could derive that same benefit from learning to listen—and voilà!—a potential benefit for learning to listen.

Another simple way to tell whether or not a benefit will be personally motivating to you is to note your immediate emotional reaction when you think of it. Here's an example. Let's say the next potential benefit of learning to be a better listener that occurs to you is that your boss will be pleased; you remember she's given you feedback about needing to listen better. Then, you'd notice whether considering that benefit moves your "emotional needle." In other words, when you reflect on your boss being happy about your improved listening, does it make you feel more inspired, excited, or interested in learning to listen? If so, great—focusing on that benefit will support your learning. If not—that is, if your emotional reaction, when you think of that potential benefit, is either neutral (*whatever*) or negative (*yuck*)—then that benefit won't pump up your aspiration. Let's say you then think of another benefit; you realize that improving your listening skills will help you to be a better parent to your kids. Perhaps your immediate emotional reaction to that potential benefit is positive (*that would be great!*). Bingo—that benefit is meaningful to you.

Think of and write down two or three potential benefits of learning the skill you've chosen that are personally meaningful to you; they may arise from other benefits that you know have motivated you to learn things in the past, or they may be new ones that create a positive emotional reaction in you when you consider them.

The personal benefits I find most motivating as I consider learning this skill or capability:

Great—you've identified a couple of things that you, personally, hope to gain from learning this new skill. Now we're going to ramp up your aspiration even more, by envisioning a future in which you're experiencing those benefits.

If you remember, in chapter 4 I taught you a process for envisioning a positive future where you're reaping the benefits of having learned your new skill. Just to remind you, that process gives you a way to put yourself into a mental time machine and create a really clear mental picture of how you'll benefit from learning this skill—one that's both realistic and motivating to you.

We've found, over the years, that envisioning a future in which your hard work has paid off and you're benefitting from your new skills has a hugely positive impact on aspiration. Once you can clearly imagine the good things that will happen for you as a result of your learning, you'll generally have enough aspiration to move forward.

Let's try it with the topic you're focusing on in this chapter.

Envisioning a "hoped-for future" where I'm reaping the benefits of my learning...

Pick a time frame (when you will be much more skilled or knowledgeable in this area).

Imagine yourself in that future, and then describe what success looks and feels like (how you feel and what you're doing, having gained the benefits from this learning).

Select the key elements (two or three sentences that best capture the benefits you're experiencing in this future world of successful learning).

Before we go on to focus on your neutral self-awareness, spend a minute luxuriating in the vision you've created of a successful future where you've learned the skill or capability you've targeted, and are experiencing the benefits of having done so. For our earlier example, of learning to listen better, that reflection might go something like this: *When my employees come to me with problems, I really understand what they're saying and help them come to their own good solutions. They respect me and see me as a skillful, supportive manager. At home, I can tell my kids feel loved and excited when I focus fully on what they're saying to me.*

When we can see ourselves in a future where we're gaining

benefits that are important to us, we want to do the things that will make that future a reality. Our aspiration increases.

Do you feel yourself now wanting to learn the skill you've targeted more than you did before? If not, you may not have chosen benefits that were personally important to you, or you may not have clearly envisioned a future where you'd be experiencing those benefits. If your aspiration hasn't increased, you may want to go back to the beginning of this section and try again—look for more personally meaningful benefits or work through the four steps of the "envisioning" process again.

And if you truly can't find the aspiration you need to learn the skill or capability you're targeting, and it's critical to your success in some part of your life, you may need to choose another path for yourself, one where learning this skill isn't essential. Because, at the end of the day, we really only do those things that we want to do more than any other option that's available to us. And if you can't get yourself to want to learn something enough to make the effort to learn it, you'd better find a road to success that doesn't include learning that thing.

That last paragraph is meant as a reality check. There are times when you simply can't make yourself want to do something. And if that thing is so deeply uninteresting to you that you just can't make yourself want to learn it, and if learning it is key to success on your current path, you may want to reconsider your path. A few years ago my husband, who had been an IT executive for almost twenty years, realized that he simply couldn't find the aspiration to learn many of the new things that were key to his continued success in the field. When he had gotten into IT, it was a burgeoning field with a kind of pioneering feel to it. He even wrote a number of books about how to use this new thing called the Internet, and helped three different organizations build their IT structures and programs from scratch.

By 2012, he found himself less and less interested in the current focus of corporate IT (data security and knowledge management, for instance). Finally, he acknowledged his inability to find the necessary level of aspiration to continue growing, and he left his job to start a craft brewery, something in which he is deeply interested. I see his aspiration every day: he bounces out of bed, raring to go, excited about learning. He now has a fully operational microbrewery, and has developed a group of delicious, award-winning craft beers. There's no way around it: aspiration is the essential fuel for new learning.

Building Neutral Self-Awareness

Let's assume you were able to ramp up your aspiration (or that you started with a workable level of aspiration), and you now feel ready to learn in this area you've chosen. It's time to focus on yourself, and get very clear on where you're starting from in your learning.

When we worked on neutral self-awareness in chapter 5, I introduced you to two powerful and interconnected skills: managing your self-talk and becoming a fair witness. I hope you've been playing around with these things, noticing how you talk to yourself about yourself and then questioning your assumptions about yourself, to find out whether they're accurate and neutral.

Before we focus on using these skills to build your neutral self-awareness about your current capabilities in the learning area you've chosen, I want to bring in something from the fourth ANEW skill—willingness to be bad first—that will help you.

Often, when we are honest enough with ourselves to recognize a weakness and clearly acknowledge it in our self-talk (e.g., *I'm a pretty poor listener right now—I interrupt a lot, and I say "I got it" rather than really making sure I understand*), our self-talk immediately leaps to a dire "fixed mindset" prediction: *And I'll never get any better.*

I just want to remind you here that you can use the self-talk of self-belief that you learned in the "Willngness to Be Bad First" chapter to counter that self-talk. That is, you can respond to that negative, unsupportive assertion in your head by thinking something hopeful and accurate like, *Wait a minute—I've gotten better at lots of things, including other interpersonal skills. For instance, I'm much better at giving others credit for their work than I used to be.*

I wanted to remind you of this because those dire predictions in our heads are what make it most painful and difficult to acknowledge our weaknesses. Knowing you can replace those negative messages with realistic "self-belief" self-talk can be very empowering.

Okay. Put on your fair witness robes and be as accurate as possible about where you're starting from in your learning about the topic you've chosen. In your notebook, or using your PDF, make two lists.

Current Strengths/Assets in This Area	Current Weaknesses/Gaps in This Area

- Review what you've written and ask: *Is my self-talk accurate?*
- If you're not sure about some things, note them and ask: *What facts do I have to support my point of view?*
- Use your answers to revise your lists, to make them as "fair witness" as possible.
- Note any self-talk you recognize that reflects strong feelings you have about either your strengths or your weaknesses—it's important to be accurate about those, too.
- Finally, if you find yourself making negative self-talk predications based on your current weaknesses, revise them, using the "self-talk of self-belief."

Let's assume that what you've written is now as clear as you can be at this moment about where you're starting from in this area of learning. Therefore, it's time to call on your sources.

> Choose a source who sees you clearly in this area of learning, wants the best for you, and is willing to be honest:

Reach out to your selected source and ask for her help in seeing yourself clearly. Remember to provide context, especially if you haven't yet called upon this person to serve as a source for you.

Show your source what you've written about your current strengths and weaknesses in this area, and invite her honest feedback. Reassure the person that you really do want honesty, and that you're open to whatever she has to say. Explore your source's areas of agreement with your self-perception, as well as areas where you disagree. Be sure to listen fully, and thank your source for the insights and honesty (particularly if they were hard to hear!). Revise what you've written as needed.

Now you have a really clear starting point for your learning: you see and acknowledge your current strengths and weaknesses and how you feel about them. I encourage you to keep checking in with yourself and with your source as you learn in this area. As you build your strengths and overcome or reduce your gaps and weaknesses, it's possible to drift into inaccuracy. For example, we've seen in coaching that some coachees improve a little and then believe that they've improved dramatically, while others have a hard time acknowledging any gains they've made.

Before we go on, I want to congratulate you: being accurate about yourself in this way requires fearlessness and self-confidence, and is key to any kind of high-payoff learning. For some people, it's difficult to acknowledge weaknesses, or fears about those weaknesses. For others, it's difficult to fully acknowledge strengths—they may have self-talk that admonishes them against "bragging" or "being too proud." I want to assure you that even though it may feel scary or uncomfortable to be this objective about yourself to begin with, the more you do it, the more you'll experience the freedom, relief, and clarity that come from acknowledging and accepting yourself as you are right now.

Re-engaging Endless Curiosity

I believe this is the most fun ANEW skill. Finding your aspiration and building your neutral self-awareness are absolutely necessary to real learning, and when you really want to do something or when you truly see yourself clearly, there's a deep satisfaction that arises, but getting to that point can feel like hard work.

Re-engaging your curiosity is, simply put, a joy.

I believe this is because becoming curious, and then satisfying that curiosity, is the opposite of being bored, jaded, uninterested, or disengaged, all of which feel pretty terrible to us. If you believe, like the scientists John Medina references in *Brain Rules*, that curiosity is a drive in us as strong as the ones for hunger, thirst, and sex, then it makes complete sense that it would feel so good. That's the nature of things that are deeply wired into us, that support our survival— they feel great, so that we'll keep doing them.

Reminding yourself of that—of how good it feels to be curious about something and to satisfy that curiosity through investigation and action—will help pull you through those times when you're convinced that you can only be bored. I'm encouraging you (you may have realized this already) to incorporate this understanding into your self-talk. So when your mind says, *Oh my god, this is so boring, I'll never learn this,* you can revise that to, *It may seem boring, but it would feel really good to get curious about this—much better than being bored. I wonder I if I can do that?*

With that in mind, I encourage you to take a pass at crafting some good curiosity questions to insert into your self-talk as you approach learning the area you've chosen—and determining some actions you can take to pursue the answers to your questions.

> Create two or three "How," "Why," or "I wonder" questions about this new area of learning, questions to which you actually want to find the answers.
>
> Now, decide an easy-for-you action that you could take to pursue the answer to each question above.

The questions and actions above should give you a good momentum toward learning in this area you've chosen. I suspect these initial questions will lead to more as you continue to learn and improve—that's the nature of curiosity.

I hope you're also playing around with "feeding the fire" of your curiosity daily, asking curious questions to yourself—or, even more bravely, aloud—about anything and everything that's important to you. I can't stress enough the idea that making curiosity an integral part of your everyday life will equip you as nothing else can to succeed in a rapidly changing world. For example, I was just speaking with a new client last week, someone who has been brought in as the head of creative for a respected children's brand that has lost its luster (and is losing its revenues). She has realized that the single most difficult thing about working with her staff to solve their problems is that they are incurious. Their mental energy is focused on defending the status quo and explaining why their brand is still better than anyone else's in the kids' space…even if the public isn't recognizing it. She sees that if she (and we) can help them get curious about why the brand's not working as well as it did and how they might need to change it, and get them to start wondering what would happen if they tried some new things—then they have a shot at bringing the brand into the twenty-first century. And that's not just true of them: it's true of all of us. If we can approach the new with our unfettered childhood curiosity, we're giving ourselves the best possible chance to keep up with the ever-accelerating rate of change that's a big part of all of our daily lives.

Becoming Willing to Be Bad First

Of course, we have to also be willing to be bad first. As I've noted throughout our time together, of the four ANEW skills, this is the most challenging for most people. And it's especially tough at work, because when you have to be bad in public, it definitely raises the degree of difficulty significantly.

One way to make it easier to be bad in front of other people is to infuse your self-talk about being bad first with accurate and supportive acknowledgments about the situation in which you have to learn. For example, in a circumstance where you're going to be in the position of being not good at something in front of your employees, rather than create the normal be bad first self-talk: *I'm going to be bad at this to begin with, and I know I can get better,* you might tweak your acceptance and self-belief self-talk to support yourself even more effectively in this particular situation: *I'm going to be bad at this to begin with—and I'll need to work on being okay with doing that around my employees. If I stay curious and confident about my ability to start as a novice and get better, that will be a powerful positive model for them.*

In fact, now that you're getting better at managing your self-talk, you can use your self-talk skills to help you deal with all the negative, unhelpful self-talk that may arise in you around being a novice. To support you in that effort, here's a handy-dandy chart of some of the more common self-talk that comes up in "being bad" situations. Trust me, you're not alone—we've heard these all before, both in our own heads and from our clients.

Unsupportive self-talk about "being bad"	Supportive (and more accurate) alternatives
I feel like a loser.	Everybody is bad at things to begin with, even people who are smart and accomplished.
I hate this.	Yeah, it's no fun to be bad at things. But it will get easier.
I can just fake it.	If I acknowledge my "novice-ness" now, I can actually learn—then I won't have to fake it.
Everybody will think I'm dumb.	People will probably think I'm confident, especially when I get better fast.
I'll get fired.	Really? Do I have any data to support that belief?
I'm actually very good at this.	That's not true—I'm just trying to avoid acknowledging my current "badness."
This isn't that important—I don't really need to learn it.	That's my fear (discomfort/anxiety) talking—I actually do need to learn this. I've gotten good at lots of things in my life—I can get better at this.

By this time, you've probably gotten pretty clear on your own particular flavors of resistance to being bad first (given your increased level of neutral self-awareness). So knowing yourself as you now do, think about the situation within which you'll have to "be bad" when learning your chosen skill (i.e., With colleagues or in private? With people who are more skilled than you or with other novices? Quickly or over a long period of time?).

Now, using the examples above as thought starters, come up with "being bad first" self-talk that's custom-tailored to overcome your specific unhelpful self-talk and to support you in your particular situation.

My "accepting not-good" self-talk for learning my chosen skill.

My self-belief self-talk for learning this skill.

If you've been playing with these ANEW skills and trying them out in various aspects of your life, you may already have experienced what I'm about to tell you. Remember when I taught you the self-talk model of *recognize, record, rethink, repeat?* Changing your self-talk about being bad is where "repeat" is going to come in really handy. For most of us, our unhelpful self-talk around being novices is particularly sticky and insistent: we've been talking to ourselves about how much we hate being bad at things and/or how we'll never get better at them for most of our lives. Those mental habits are like an old (bumpy) road that we've driven down over and over again.

Substituting your alternative, more supportive and accurate self-talk is like making a new road and then driving on that. After a while the new road will be the default route, but it can take some time. So don't get impatient with yourself if you have to keep consciously shifting your self-talk, in learning situations, toward acceptance of not-good and self-belief. It will get easier. And you can employ some of the physical techniques we discussed in the last chapter, too. If you find yourself stuck in not accepting your novice state or not believing that you can get better, take a deep breath, relax your shoulders and hands, and raise your chin. Remind yourself that you're going to be bad at your chosen skill to begin with, and then you'll get better at it. Take another deep breath...

Now on to the final element of ANEW: bridging. You're good at lots of things. Everyone is. Because we've learned so many skills and capabilities throughout our lives, when we're faced with learning something new, it's rare to have that thing be completely unlike anything we've ever learned before. It's not impossible, but it is uncommon.

Given that, we usually have skills and knowledge we can bridge from when learning in a new area. However, it's particularly important that we bring our fair witness and curiosity skills to bear in this endeavor—it's way too easy to "over-bridge" and assume something new is more like things we already know than it actually is.

In coaching and teaching executives over the years, and in observing my own learning process, I've come to realize that over-bridging is simply another way for our minds to avoid being bad first. For example, a few years ago, I was coaching an executive who is very, very smart, and is a pretty good business operator but a poor delegator. He had been given a big new job, running a division of his company, and wasn't doing well at it; his direct reports, who were quite senior, were frustrated about his level of involvement in their decisions, and all felt they were capable of a greater degree of autonomy (they were). I'd gotten him to a point of workable neutral self-awareness—he acknowledged he wasn't great at letting go.

As I prepared to teach him our model for delegating, he noted that he thought it would be pretty easy, because (in his words) it was just about giving clear direction, which he was good at doing. I agreed that he was very clear in his direction—but then I asked how he thought the two were alike.

"Oh, you know," he said, "as long as you let people know what's expected of them, that's really the heart of delegation. Right?"

"Well," I responded, "clarity on the area you're delegating is one aspect of delegation, yes. There's quite a bit more to it than that..."

"Yeah," he interrupted, "but that's the main thing, isn't it? I probably just need to be clearer about what I need them to do."

It took me a good deal of time and effort to detach him from his conviction that giving clear direction—which he knew how to do—was pretty much identical to delegation. But finally he was able to realize that, while his skills of being direct, succinct, and clear were things he could build on in delegating, there were a number of other skills he didn't yet have that he would need to learn in order to be able to delegate well (perhaps the most important being the skill of letting people actually complete the work on their own, once he had delegated it to them!).

After he learned to delegate, and was having some success, he said to me, "You know, I think I was just trying to feel like I was already pretty good at delegating, or that it wouldn't take much to learn it." A great insight.

So, as you think about which skills you can bridge from in learning this new skill that you've chosen, focus on staying curious and accurate (fair witness), and you'll be able to build strong bridges that will actually speed your learning.

Pick a skill or capability you already have that you believe may be related to your chosen topic. Go beyond the obvious in thinking about which of your current skills might support your learning in this new area. For example, a stay-at-home mom going back into the job world might initially think that very little of her "mom" skills are related to her new job as a coordinator. But the skills she's developed in time management and organization could be very bridgeable. They're not exactly the same, because her job will also require her to deal with people at her level and above in the organization in diplomatic and politically astute ways (versus herding three-year-olds), and she'll have to learn to follow the policies and processes of her new company. However, the core skills—of having to accomplish a number of tasks within a certain period of time, under continually changing circumstances—are very similar.

So cast your net of reflection wide, and think of a possible bridging topic.

Now ask yourself: *How is this skill or capability similar to and different from what might be required in the new situation?*

Here's one added safeguard against over-bridging that I've found very helpful. As you're learning this new topic or skill, if you find yourself thinking, *Oh, this is just like that other thing I know,* flip that self-talk into a question: *Is this just like that other thing I know?* That will immediately shift you from conclusion to curiosity, opening your mind to observe how the two are actually similar and different, and allowing you to then leverage your previous learning in helpful and realistic ways.

And Finally...

If we were in a coaching session together, I'd look at you now and ask, "So, do you feel you have what you need to take these skills back into your life and use them?" And if you said yes, we'd agree on how to reconnect to check your progress and celebrate your success. And if you said no, I'd ask what wasn't clear and we'd spend some more time talking or practicing.

We don't have that luxury, so I'll direct you toward two resources to support your learning and your use of these skills. First, please continue to use this book as a reference. I've written it as a handbook to help you develop these critical skills for succeeding in today's world. Dip in and out, redo the activities, think about what you've read; bounce your thoughts off others and engage them in the process. In addition, you can also go to proteusleader.com, where you'll find curated video, audio, and written resources about the ANEW skills organized under the "Be Bad First" area, as well as other management and leadership topics.

Thank you for your time and focus: I hope you use these ANEW skills to create a fascinating and successful life for yourself in this time of constant change. I'll leave you with a final thought from our fellow learner and master of mastery Michelangelo, an encouragement to keep going toward the new and breaking through the limitations you place upon yourself:

The greater danger for most of us lies not in setting our aim too high and falling short; but in setting our aim too low, and achieving our mark.

—Michelangelo

ACKNOWLEDGMENTS

So many people have been instrumental to the creation of these ideas and this book:

First, to my partner in business-building, possibility-envisioning, and true friendship, Jeff Mitchell. I hope you feel as appreciated by me as I do by you. Thank you so much for being on this journey with me.

To my wonderful agent, Jim Levine, with whom I began to frame this book—and who gave me simple, honest feedback about the badness of my first effort. Thank you for your insight, honesty, and quiet enthusiasm.

To my first-ever research assistant, Mollie West, who found me lots of knowledge gems, and started me thinking down paths that led to lots of others. Thank you.

To everyone at Bibliomotion: I've found my publishing home. I'm really glad, Erika and Jill, that you followed your entrepreneurial spirit and that you invited me into your endeavor. So fun figuring out this new century of publishing with you.

To Barbara Cave Henricks, Megan Grajeda, and Rusty Shelton: you guys are the best in the business, hands-down, and it's always a joy and an honor to team with you.

To my fellow Proteans: We're creating a great thing, and I feel proud of what we do individually and together—and so excited that we support each other to be a living laboratory for all the ANEW skills every day. I know you'll use all of this to help our clients.

To Rachel, Ian and Kate: thank you for being so cool, and for letting me support your success. You'll never know how much of what you've taught me has ended up in here and in everything I do.

To Patrick: for every single thing.

NOTES

Chapter 1

1. Lesley Partridge, *Creating Competitive Advantage with HRM* (Select Knowledge Limited, 1999), 128.
2. Robert Terry, "Accountability Needed for Workplace Training," *Financial Times*, December 12, 2011.
3. Jennifer S. Mueller, Shimul Melwani, and Jack A. Goncalo, "The Bias Against Creativity: Why People Desire but Reject Creative Ideas," Cornell University ILR School Site, http://digitalcommons.ilr.cornell.edu/articles/450.
4. James S. Atherton, "Resistance to Learning: A Discussion Based on Participants in In-Service Professional Training Programmes," *Journal of Vocational Education and Training* 51:1 (1999): 77–90.
5. Atherton, "Resistance to Learning."

Chapter 2

1. Andrew K. Przybylski, C. Scott Rigby, and Richard M. Ryan, "A Motivational Model of Video Game Engagement," *Review of General Psychology* 14:2 (2010): 154–166.
2. John Medina, *Brain Rules* (Seattle: Pear Press, 2008), 271.

Chapter 5

1. David A. Dunning, Chip Heath, and Jerry M. Suls, "Flawed Self-Assessment: Implications for Health, Education, and the Workplace," *Psychological Science in the Public Interest* (2004).
2. Carol S. Dweck, *Mindset: The New Psychology of Success* (New York: Random House, 2006).

3. Eric S. Harter, *The Quest for Sustainable Leadership: The Importance of Connecting Leadership Principles to Concepts of Organizational Sustainability* (Weatherhead School of Management, Case Western Reserve University, 1999).

Chapter 6

1. Medina, *Brain Rules,* 264–265.

Chapter 7

1. Megan McArdle, *The Up Side of Down: Why Failing Well Is the Key to Success* (New York: Viking, 2014), 1–2.

Chapter 8

1. Pamela K. Adlemann and R. B. Zajonc, "Facial Efference and the Experience of Emotion," *Annual Review of Psychology* (1989).

REFERENCES

Atherton, James S. "Resistance to Learning: A Discussion Based on Participants in In-Service Professional Training Programmes." *Journal of Vocational Education and Training* 51:1 (1999): 77–90.

Dunning, David A., Chip Heath, and Jerry M. Suls. "Flawed Self-Assessment: Implications for Health, Education, and the Workplace." *Psychological Science in the Public Interest* (2004).

Dweck, Carol S. *Mindset: The New Psychology of Success.* New York: Random House, 2006.

Fuller, Buckminster R., *Critical Path,* New York: St. Martin's Press, 1981.

Harter, Eric S. *The Quest for Sustainable Leadership: The Importance of Connecting Leadership Principles to Concepts of Organizational Sustainability.* Weatherhead School of Management, Case Western Reserve University, 1999.

McArdle, Megan. *The Up Side of Down: Why Failing Well Is the Key to Success.* New York: Viking, 2014.

Mueller, Jennifer S., Shimul Melwani, and Jack A. Goncalo. "The Bias Against Creativity: Why People Desire but Reject Creative Ideas." Cornell University ILR School Site. http://digitalcommons.ilr.cornell.edu/articles/450.

Partridge, Lesley. *Creating Competitive Advantage with HRM.* Select Knowledge Limited, 1999.

Pink, Daniel H. *Drive: The Surprising Truth About What Motivates Us*. New York: Riverhead Books, 2009.

Przybylski, Andrew K., C. Scott Rigby, and Richard M. Ryan "A Motivational Model of Video Game Engagement." *Review of General Psychology* 14:2 (2010): 154–166.

Terry, Robert. "Accountability Needed for Workplace Training." *Financial Times*, December 12, 2011.

INDEX

ABOUT THE AUTHOR

ERIKA ANDERSEN is the founding partner of Proteus, a coaching, consulting, and training firm that focuses on leader readiness. She and her colleagues at Proteus support leaders at all levels to get ready and stay ready to meet whatever the future might bring.

Erika advises senior executives in companies like NBCUniversal, Tory Burch, GE, Madison Square Garden, Hulu, and Viacom, focusing with them on organizational visioning and strategy, team development, and their own management and leadership evolution.

She also shares her insights about leading people, staying ready for the future, and creating successful businesses through her books and speaking engagements, and via social media. Erika is one of the most popular leadership bloggers at Forbes.com. In addition to *Be Bad First: Get Good at Things Fast to Stay Ready for the Future*, she is also the author of *Leading So People Will Follow, Being Strategic,* and *Growing Great Employees*, and the author and host of the *Proteus Leader Show*, a regular podcast that offers quick, practical support for leaders and managers.

Connect with Erika on Twitter (@erikaandersen), on Facebook (www.facebook.com/ErikaAndersen), on her own blog (erikaandersen.com), or at Forbes (www.forbes.com/sites/erikaandersen).

Now that you've read *Be Bad First*, you might want to know more about how my colleagues and I work with our clients. Proteus is a team of smart, passionate, honorable folks who bring to life the skills and ideas in my books, blogs and podcasts, as well as model and ideas of their own creation. All the work we do focuses on leader readiness: we help leaders *get ready and stay ready for whatever the future might bring.* We work in three practice areas:

Strengthening Leaders
We draw upon the model at the heart of *Leading So People Will Follow*, as well as the ideas and skills in *Growing Great Employees* and *Being Strategic*, to support leaders be more fully accepted and to better build their business. We coach leaders individual and in teams.

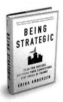

Clarifying Vision and Strategy
This is where we put our approach—outlined in the *Being Strategic* book and televisic show—into practice. We work with companies of all sizes and types to envision a successful organizational future, to craft a practical plan for getting there, and to engage their people in making it a reality.

Building Skills and Knowledge
Growing Great Employees provides clear guidance about why and how to manage well. We offer powerful, practical training programs based on the skills in this book, so that people leave our courses ready and able to manage and lead better. And we can teach our clients' trainers to get the same results.

If you'd like more support to get ready and stay ready for your own future, please go t ProteusLeader.com. Thank you so much for your interest.